FEUDATORIES UNDER EASTERN CHĀḶUKYAS

FEUDATORIES
UNDER
EASTERN CHĀḶUKYAS

(HISTORY AND CULTURE OF ANDHRAS)

Dr. K. Suryanarayana

Gian Publishing House
29/6 SHAKTI NAGAR • DELHI-110007 • INDIA

GIAN PUBLISHING HOUSE
29/6 Shakti Nagar, Delhi-110007

ISBN 81-212-0092-X

PRINTED IN INDIA
Published by Mrs. Gayatri Garg for Gian Publishing House
29/6, Shakti Nagar, Delhi-110007 and
Printed at Chauhan Printing Press, N-69/2, Gali No. 17,
Brhampuri, Delhi-110053

PREFACE

The present book is purported to present chapters on various aspects on the history and culture of the Andhras. The history of the Chāḷukyas in Andhra may be rightly stated as the history of Medieval Andhradesa for thousand years beginning with the conquest of Vengi in the first quarter of seventh century A.D. by the Bādāmi Chāḷukya king Pulakeśi II and ending with the total disappearance of the Chāḷukya authority in Andhra at the end of sixteenth century. It was in their regime that a major portion of Andhradesa was united politically and culturally. Telugu literature was born and spread in their patronage ; and the Andhras developed their own styles in the spheres of art and architecture due to their encouragement. In all their success it became necessary on their part to believe and depend upon some subordinate officers and feudal chiefs like Pattavardhanis and Katakarajas who devotedly followed them and guarded their interests. The history of those feudal families is studied in detail in the first chapter.

The chapter on Bettubeta is intended to specify his identification, which problem aroused much discussion among the scholars in the field. Chapters on the Kollipara plates and on the successors of Bēta Vijayaditya are either corrections or new interpretations to the hitherto prevailing views about them. The social status and other details of the Brahmana and Vaisya communities are thoroughly dealt with in some other chapters.

I wish to express my deep sense of gratitude to my esteemed teacher Dr. C. Somasundara Rao, Professor and Head of the Department of History and Archaeology, Andhra University whose constant encouragement and guidance stood behind all my research pursuits. His critical acumen was of particular help to me in writing some of the chapters included in this book. I am also grateful to Dr. Y. Srirama Murty, Professor of History, Andhra University, for his cooperation and for initiating me to the field of research by providing all facilities. I thank the editors of various journals where these articles were published earlier.

My thanks are due to Mr. M. Appa Rao, Steno-typist, who neatly typed the press-copy and to Gian Publishing House, Delhi, for undertaking the publication of the work and its neat and speedy execution.

Dept. of History and Archaeology,
Andhra University,
Waltair

K. SURYANARAYANA

ABBREVIATIONS

A.P.A.R.E.	:	Āndhra Pradesh Annual Report on Epigraphy
A.P.H.C.	:	Proceedings of the Āndhra Pradesh History Congress
A.R.E.	:	Annual Report on (South) Indian Epigraphy
A.S.P.P.	:	Āndhra Sāhitya Parishad Patrikā
C.T.I.	:	Corpus of Telangana Inscriptions
Epi. Āndhrica	:	Epigraphic Āndhrica
Epi. Carnātica	:	Epigraphia Carnātica
E.I.	:	Epigraphia Indica
J.A.H.R.S.	:	Journal of Āndhra Historical Research Society
J.B.B.R.A.S.	:	Journal of Bombay Branch of the Royal Asiatic Society
I.A.	:	Indian Antiquary
I.H.C.	:	Proceedings of the Indian History Congress
N.D.I.	:	Nellore District Inscriptions
Sewell's List	:	List of Antiquarian Remains in the Madras Presidency by Robert Sewell
S.I.I.	:	South Indian Inscriptions
V.R.	:	V. Rangacharya's Topographical List of Inscriptions of the Madras Presidency

TRANSLITERATION

a ā i ī u ū ṛi e ē ai o ō au aṁ aḥ
k kh g gh ṅ
ch chh j jh n
ṭ ṭh ḍ ḍh ṇ
p ph b bh m
y r l v s sh s h
Dravidian Letters : ṛ ḷ ḻ
Visarga : ḥ

CONTENTS

Preface v

Abbreviations vii

Transliteration Chart ix

Chapters

I Feudatories under Eastern Chāḷukyas 1

II Asanapura of the Chāḷukan Period 20

III The Earliest Record of the Chāḷukyas of Vēmulavāḍa 27

IV A Critical Telugu Inscription of Viriyālas 37

V Forgotten Chāḷukyan Family in Coastal Āndhra 49

VI Beta Vijayaditya ānd His Successors 57

VII Brāhmaṇas in Medieval Āndhra 66

VIII Peda Cherukuru Inscription of one Unidentified Vishṇuvardhana 76

IX Vishṇuvardhana of Vaiśyapurāṇam 87

X Vaiśyas in Medieval Āndhra 94

Bibliography 105

Index 109

1

FEUDATORIES UNDER EASTERN CHĀḶUKYAS : AN INTRODUCTION

In the history of Andhradēśa, the advent of the Eastern Chāḷukyas (A.D. 624-1075) or the Chāḷukyas of Vēṅgī is significant as marking the inauguration of a glorious period under which the culture of the Telugu people took its real shape. The matchless efforts at extension of the kingdom during the period of Raṇavikrama Pulakēśi II, the dear brother of Kubja Vishṇuvardhana who founded the Vēṅgī kingdom, brought the Eastern Chālukyas to Āndhra from the borders of Karṇāṭaka. Their march resulted in the establishment of a stable kingdom with an uninterrupted sway for more than five centuries with an unbroken line of succession. Probably with the zeal of extension of empire, their praśastīs claimed connection with Mahāsēna or Kārtikēya, the God of war, as the tutilary deity of the line. In some of their inscriptions they claimed to have occupied the whole earth by the fierce prowess of their own arms (*Sva-bhujavikrama-krānta-mahī-bhujām*).[1] Undoubtedly, in the series of their conquests it became necessary for them to depend upon some of the subordinate officers and chiefs who followed them loyally and guarded their interests throughout their political career. At the time of succession-struggles in the royal family and in subduing the rebellious elements in the kingdom, these subordinate families played a decisive role in setting their fortunes. To cite an example : in the civil war while ensued in the time of Mangalēśa in Bādāmī, it was a subordinate family that of Ādi Mahā Bappara, which helped and supported the claims of Pulakēśi II for the throne.[2] Similarly it would have been impossible for Kubjavishṇuvardhana to establish himself in Āndhradēśa, an unfamiliar area before the date of their Aihole *Praśasti*, without the willing support and hearty cooperation of some of his feudatory families. He seems to have brought him a number of military chieftains, settled them in Vēṅgīmaṇḍala, bestowed upon them rulership of small territories as rewards for the loyal military services rendered to him in the conquest of Vēṅgīnāḍu and consolidation of the Chāḷukyan authority over it. The Durjaya family of the Giripaśchimasīma was rewarded with the hereditary rulership of some villages[3] on the southern bank of the river Kṛshṇa. Similarly, even though it was not directly mentioned, the Matsya family to which Aṭavi Durjaya, the ājñaptī of the Chīpurupalli plates, belonged might have been also rewarded with the rule of a small trace of the country in northern Āndhra.[4] In this manner Chāḷukyas were prepared to honour and reward the services of these chieftains by bestowing upon them rulership over small territories. But it seems, some prestigious families, who deemed devoted service as a reward in itself, declined such favours and preferred to continue in the service of the royal family. To that noble category belonged the great warrior families, Paṭṭavardhanīs and Kaṭakarājas. These two were the prominent dynasties which devoted their lives to the services of the Eastern Chāḷukyas with unsullied loyalty and unflinching dedication.

Paṭṭavardhanīs

Mention was made about the Paṭṭavardhanī family in many inscriptions, prominent among them being the Goṇṭūru grant of Amma I (A.D. 922-929)[5] and Pāṁbaṟṟu and Kaluchumbaṟṟu grants of Amma II (A.D. 945-970).[6] In these inscriptions

Paṭṭavardhanīs traced their descent from the period of Kubjavishṇuvardhana, the founder of the Eastern Chāḷukyan kingdom.

Kāla Kaṁpa or Kōṭa Kaṁpa, the famous military general of Kubjavishṇuvardhana is stated to be the founder of the Paṭṭavardhanī family. A descendant of him was Sōmāditya, who was presumably a commander of the army under Guṇagavijayāditya. Sōmāditya's son Pṛthviyarāja, was in the service of Chāḷukya Bhīma I. His son was Bhaṇḍanāditya ; and he was connected with Kollābhigaṇḍa Vijayāditya IV and Ammarāja I. Thus the line of Paṭṭavardhanīs was closely interwoven with the history of the Chāḷukyas of Vēṅgī.

Kālakaṁpa was the first known person in the Paṭṭavardhanī family. He was a military officer under Kubjavishṇuvardhana, and he claimed to have conquered and killed the Vallabhī prince Daddara at the instance of his master. Daddara was identified with Daddara I or II of Gujarat, who overthrew some hostile Naga chiefs and acquired the territory which was in the Gaekwad's dominions.[7] After eliminating Daddara, Kālakaṁpa followed his king and came down to settle in the Vēṅgī country. From that time onwards, Paṭṭavardhanīṣ were regarded by the Chāḷukyan family as the chief promoters and supporters of the 'ever increasing fortunes' and glory of their dynasty.

Again, Paṭṭavardhanīs came into the picture in the period of Kaliyartigaṇḍa Vijayāditya IV, who ascended the Vēṅgī throne roughly three centuries after Kubjavishṇuvardhana. It looks strange that in these three centuries none of the records mentioned the details of these loyal subordinates. It was in the period of Vijayāditya IV, that Paṭṭavardhanī Bhaṇḍanāditya, who acquired the titles of 'Uggivelagauḍu' and 'Kuntāditya' by displaying marvellous heroism in the crush of the battles, is reported as "the temple of great prowess and fame" (*kīrti pratāpālayah*).[8] He was appointed commander-in-chief by Vishṇuvardhana Ammarāja I.[9]

Bhaṇḍanāditya was the son of Pṛthivīyarāja, who was the son of Sōmāditya, who again was a descendant of Kālakaṁpa of the time of Kubjavishṇuvardhana.

Even though it is not exactly known, there seemed to be some struggle for the accession to the throne on the death of Vijayāditya IV. The accession of his eldest son of Ammarāja I was opposed by some of the dāyādas and feudatory commanders with the help of the neighbouring Rāshṭrakūṭas. In an inscription of Ammarāja I, he himself mentioned that[10] he had to use his sword against his feudatory relatives and commanders "who had joined that party of his natural adversaries". His actual words in the inscriptions are—

......Ripu-timi
rān-nihatya prakriti-sapatna-nikshipta-sāmanta-kulya
kuṭila-manōbhaṅga-karam karavālam-uttkriṣya-śakatītraya
sampannapratāpā varjita-pitṛ-pitāmaha
Prakṛti-balah......

What happened at this juncture is not exactly known. There could be doubt that there was a civil war in the country, and the dāyādas who claimed the throne and the dishonest and treacherous commanders entered into a conspiracy and joined hands with the Rāshṭrakūṭas, the natural enemies of the Vēṅgī Chāḷukyas. Here some scholars argue that Bhaṇḍanāditya of the Paṭṭavardhanī family was one among the commanders who changed their loyalties in this period of political cataclysm.[11] But such questionable conduct was against the very grain of the Paṭṭavardhanīs. They never tried to prevent the accession of the Chāḷukyan princes. They stood by them always. They were first and foremost in supporting the wishes of their overloards and in helping them to realise their dreams. From the earliest times, their family was closely attached to the royal house in unflinching loyalty and enjoyed their trust and received recognition and rewards. Bhaṇḍanāditya too served the Chāḷukyas from the time of Amma I's father. In the above mentioned inscription Ammarāja I himself extolled Bhaṇḍanāditya and the Paṭṭavardhanī family in endearing and flattering terms :[12]

......Asamat-kula-kalyāṇa-paramparā-niyōg - ādhikṛta-paṭṭa-varddhini-vaṁśā-graṇyā/Kōṭa (?) *kampaiti viśrutē-na kubja-*

vishṇuvarddhan-ānucharēṇa sangrāmē tad anujñayā/durdharsha balaṁ daṭṭara-nā
mānaṁ vinihatya ta-chchinhāniyēna jagṛhirē/tat kula-prasūta sōmādityasya sūnur-a
nēka-yuddha·labdha-pratāpaḥ pṛtivīya rājaḥ/Tat-sūnus-sakalārāti-mada chchēda-karā-
Yudhaḥ sēvakō Vijayāditya-Kalīyatyāṁka-bhūbhujaḥ-ābhaishur-Bhaṇḍanādityam ḍṛshṭvā-
Prītim-Upārjanaṁ prāptam-ujvala-gaṇṭākamyamparē yama-sannibham/yōhi/śatrūṇāṁ-
Tumulēshu Vīra-paṭāham samśrāvya jitvābalam kuntāditya iśrut-ānkita-mahā-kīrti pratāp-ālavah/mat-chittam paritōshya bhṛtya padavīṁ-labdhvā prasāda-gantaḥ sphīt-ā-
nēka-bal-āri-bhūpa vijayī-śrī-janma bāhunnatīḥ......

Such lavish praise could not have been bestowed on a dishonest deserter and vile traitor. On the other hand, the friendship of this Bhaṇḍanāditya, who was equal to God Yama in power, and the sound of whose war-drums struck terror and despair in his enemies, was sought by Ammarāja I at the most critical period of his political career and was given the manificent help in a liberal and unreserved manner. As pointed out, it is the mistake of the critics when they estimate this Bhaṇḍanāditya as a dishonest and treacherous commander. In fact, he pleased the King's mind and obtained his favour. As a reward of recognition of his glorious service, Ammarāja gave him the village of Goṇṭūru together with the rulership of twelve more villages in the kaṇḍēruvāṭi *vishaya,* and besides honoured him with the rank of the general of the army.

The lineage of the Paṭṭavardhanīs known from inscriptions is as under :

Kōṭa Kaṁpa
or
Kāla Kaṁpa
|
Sōmāditya
|
Pṛthivīyarāja
|
Bhaṇḍanāditya

Mention may be made in this context of one Ballāladēva Vēlabhaṭa Boḍḍiya who figured in the period of Vijayāditya Ammarāja II, the most glorious personality in the Eastern Chāḷukyan history. Ballāladēva was the son of a lady Pammava of the Paṭṭavardhanī family.[13] The relation of Ballāladēva and Pammava to the above-mentioned lineage is not known. Except Ballāladēva's mother's name, no other details of them are known.

But some scholars interpreted the omission of the name of Ballāladeva's father and other details as due to the fact that lady Pammava belonged to the class of courtesans attached to the royal harem by virtue of a hereditary right and custom[14] and so could not have enjoyed the status of a married woman. All the same, she could have claimed the family name of her patron for her son Ballāladēva. The Masulipatnam grant of Ammarāja II states how he anointed Paṭṭavardhanī Ballāladēva as the heir-apparent of the Vēṅgī throne. It is also said that he was made a commander of an army of two thousand horse and elephant troups and he had the honour of using a white parasol and a white Balaka-piñchha, the *insignia* associated with status of the yuvarāja.[15] These were the rare and unıque honours for a servant of the kingdom. Ammarāja granted some lands to Ballāladēva ; and this Ballāladēva acted as the *ājñapatī* for some of the grants.[16]

As a courtesan and as a favourite mistress of Ammarāja, a beautiful young lady Chāmekāṁba, of the Paṭṭavardhanī family is known from the Kaluchumbaṟṟu grant of Amma II.[17] This record registers the grant of a village Kaluchumbaṟṟu in the Attilināḍu province, to a Jain teacher named Arhanandin, belonging to the Velahariganạ and the Aḍḍākaligachcha, for the purpose of providing for repairs to the charitable dining hall of Jain temple called Sarvalōkāśraya Jina Bhavana. This grant was issued at the instance of Chāmekāṁba of the Paṭṭavardhanīs, the mistress of the King and a pupil of Arhanandin.

In the inscription the lady is described[18] as—

......Śrī-rāja-chaluky-ānvaya-parivarita-paṭṭavardhikā-nvaya-tilaka/ganikājana-mukha-kamala dyumaṇi-dyutir-ihahi-chāmekāṁb-ā bhuta-sa//-dharmma-jala vivarddhana......

Chāmekāṁba was a Jainaśrāvakī, who claimed to be a gaṇika herself.

Further, there is every possibility to identify this Paṭṭavardhanī Chāmekāṁa with Sāmekāṁba (?) who was mentioned in the Āruṁbāka plates of Bādapa.[19] Āruṁbāka plates are more useful in bringing the Paṭṭavardhanī family into more light. The donee of this grant was Gaṇḍanārāyaṇa, the famous archer and son of Nṛpakāma. This Nṛpakāma was the benevolent ruler of the territory surrounding the lake Kollēru in Āndhra, and his daughter was given in marriage to Ammarāja Vijayāditya II.[20] Nāyamāṁba, the wife of Nṛpakāma was the elder sister of Chāmekāṁba. As such there was every possibility to identify Chāmekāṁba with her namesake of the Paṭṭavardhanī family. Her son was Chandena. The relation between Paṭṭavardhanī family and the family of Bhaṇḍanāditya is given hereunder.

Bālāditya — Paṭṭavardhanī family

Nṛpakāma + Nāyamāṁba — Chāmekāṁba

Wife of Amma II — Gaṇḍanārāyaṇa — Chandena

Viewed in this perspective Chāmekāṁba stood in the position of the sister of Ammarāja II's mother-in-law. In what circumstances she managed to become a favourite mistress of the same Ammarāja and in what conditions she converted herself into a Jainaśrāvakī are not known. But the known fact was both Chandena and Gaṇḍanārāyaṇa played prominent roles in a civil war which threw the reign of Ammarāja II into confusion.

B.V. Krishna Rao opined that even though the name of the Paṭṭavardhanī family was not specifically mentioned in inscriptions, Chellava and Nāgipōtī of the period of Chāḷukya Bhīma I also belonged to this family.[21] Chellava, a musician and dancer, was the favourite courtesan of Chāḷuka Bhīma I. In the words of Chāḷukya Bhīma, she was a *samasta gāndharva vidyā vēdinī*.[22]

Her father was Mallapa, an artist who was compared to the celestial musician Tuṁbura. The grand mother of this Chellava was Tuṇḍaka, a lady of uncomparable beauty and charm.

The above mentioned Nāgipōtī was the wet-nurse of Chāḷukya Bhīma I. She was described in the Drujjūru grant[23] as :

> ......*Chāḷukya Bhīma-bhūpāla-dhāttrī(trī) dhāti-īva-chāpura-kshmayā kshtriya prāyā nāgipōtir-iti-śruta//A sīt-tasyāssutā Gāmakāṁbānām-Āṁbika-sama/matu(ḥ) stanyaṁ samī kṛtya Bhī-*
> *ma-rājēna yā pappu//S-ājījanat-kumāram śaktiyuktaṁ kumara Tat/Bhima-raja-*
> *sya sēnānyaṁ/Mahākālam......*

Mahākāla was the commander of the armies of Chāḷukya Bhīma. He was the son of Gāmakāṁba, the foster sister of the king. Chāḷukya Bhīma I had shared along with Gāmakāṁba, the milk of her mother Nāgipōtī. The word 'Pōtī' was a respectable name-ending in those days. Nāgipōtī was described as the (foster) second mother of the king. Mahākāla's services were greatly remembered even after the death of Chāḷukya Bhīma and were rewarded by a grant of the village Drujjūṛu by Bhīma's grandson Vishṇuvardhana Ammarāja I.[24]

Whatever might be the status they acquired they came nearer to the royal family in their devotion and rendered memorable services. Ammarāja I himself declared—

> "The Paṭṭavardhanīs were the foremost among the favourites of the kings of Vēṅgī, because they were able to secure the constant prosperity and victory of the Chāḷukyas".[25]

Kaṭakarājas

Another loyal subordinate family that served the Vēṅgī Chāḷukyan rulers, in no less measure than the Paṭṭavardhanī family, was the Kaṭakarāja family. Loyal and devoted services to the sovereign paved the rise of this family, became famous commanders and trusted officials and laboured to protect the fame and dignity of their overlords. Though Brahmins by birth, they chose, like many others of their community, the profession of arms as a means of livelihood. As educated members of the community, their help was indispensable to the state in administration as well and consequently they were encouraged to accept lucrative posts under the Vēṅgī Chāḷukyan Government. For the first time, they appeared prominently in the period of Samastabhuvanāśraya Guṇaga Vijayāditya, the greatest prince of the Vēṅgī Chāḷukyan dynasty.

Guṇaga Vijayāditya, as he proudly declared, reigned over a vast kingdom which included the whole of the *dakshiṇāpatha*, together with the province of Trikaḷiṅga, for forty-four years.[26] In those days, he was popularly known by his appellations in Telugu, 'Tribhuvanānkuśuḍu' and 'Bejayuḍu'. In fact, the greatness and the height of glory and power which the Vēṅgī Chāḷukyan empire attained in his reign was never reached nor approached either before him or after him. This family started its political career under the auspices of such a great monarch.

Inscriptions form the main source of the history of this Kaṭakarāja family. Inscriptions of Addanki[27], Dharmavaram,[28] Sāṭalur,[29] Uṛuṭūru,[30] Masulipatam,[31] Chiṁbulūru[32] and Pōnaṅgi[33] in the period of Guṇagavijayāditya ; inscriptions at Dharmavaram[34] and Mōga plates[35] during the reign of Chāḷukya Bhīma I, and Maliyaṁpūḍi[36] and Nāgiyaṁpūḍi plates[37] during Ammarāja Vijayāditya II's rule are important among them.

Kaḍeyarāja was the first noteworthy person of this family. Scholars opined that the word 'Kaḍeyaraja' was the vernacular corruption of 'Kaṭakarāja', which might be the designation of his office and not his personal name.[38] He was the grandson of Bhaṭṭakāla. His father's name is not known. As a most powerful and trusted general he served his master faithfully for several years. But in an expedition against rebel feudatories, it appears that he was killed on the battlefield ; and thus he spent his life, to its last breath in the service of his youthful master. Pōnaṅgi and Chiṁbulūru plates refer to this fact.

Parachakrēṇa yudhvājaudattaprāṇasya bhūbhurutē sūnuh kaḍeyarājasya paṇḍarangō guṇādhikhah

B.V. Krishna Rao observed that Kaḍeyarāja was killed in the wars with the rebel Bōya Chieftains of the South.[39] M. Somasekhara Sarma was of the opinion that Kaḍeyarāja died in the period before the campaign on Bōya Koṭṭams.[40] Krishna Sastry suggested that Kaḍeyarāja might have been killed in the campaign carried on against Maṅgi, Sankila, and Rāshṭrakūṭa Kṛshṇarāja.[41] But in the absence of evidence we might place Kaḍeyarāja's death in the period before the campaign against Bōya Chieftains. His son was the famous general Paṇḍaraṅga. A broken inscription from Dharmavaram reports another son of Kaḍeyarāja, Ayyapayya.[42]

Vijayāditya pāda/padma bhramarāyamāṇa śrīmatkaḍeyarāju guṇa gaṇābharanuṇḍu dana/ke. ni Ēśvarunakuṁ Gārtikēy-uṇḍuṁbōle choushashṭikalā viśāraduṇḍayna/Ayyapayyayu-

But his other details are not known.

After the death of Kaḍeyarāja, his son Paṇḍaraṅga was anointed as the commander-in-chief of the entire Chāḷukyan army. In the very first year of his assumption of office he was entrusted with the duty of bringing the rebel Bōyas to their knees. The Dharmavaram inscription of Chāḷukya Bhīma I mentioned that the revolt made by the Bōyas was the cause of this invasion.[43] But Paṇḍaraṅga in his Addanki inscription declared that this expedition was intended just to exhibit what strength and valour the king had (*balagarva moppa*).[44] Paṇḍaraṅga was the most reputed general of his age ; and it is no exaggeration to say that the fame of Guṇagavijayāditya as a conqueror rested in no small measure on the outstanding military genius and achievements of Paṇḍaraṅga. Chiṁbulūru grant eulogised him as the general, who was honoured with a seat by the side of the king when weighed against gold (*svāminā saha yōgēna hēma bhāra tulā duritah*).[45] N. Venkataramanayya observed that Paṇḍaraṅga was the fighting arm of his master and most of the victories, usually ascribed in the inscriptions to Guṇaga Vijayāditya, were actually won by him.[46]

As stated already, Paṇḍaraṅga's Addanki inscription mentioned how his marches against the territories of the Bōya chieftains who had apparently revolted against the sovereignty of Vēṅgī were intended to demonstrate how powerful and mighty the king was. It is not known who these Bōyas were. They might possibly be the feudatory chieftains of Bāṇa, Alūpa, Gaṅga, Chōḍa, and the Vaidumba families who ruled in the southern Āndhra country as vassals of the Eastern Chāḷukyas. Probably this Bōya revolt was a part and parcel of the conflict between the Pallavas and Vēṅgī Chāḷukyas. Paṇḍaraṅga conquered and destroyed the twelve impreganable Koṭṭams of the Bōyas and re-established the Eastern Chāḷukyan suzerainty over the new area. On the way he dismantled the fort of Kattem, the Kaṭṭepu-durgamu, which was identified by the government epigraphist as Kāṭhivaram in the Tenali Taluque.[47] But B.V. Krishna Rao rejected the suggestion and tried to locate it somewhere in the Toṇḍaimaṇḍalam and Vaidumbavāḍi which corresponded to the parts of Rāyalasīma in Andhra Pradesh.[48] According to K.V. Lakshmana Rao there was every possibility to trace the place to the Nallamalai hills.[49] But still more research is necessary to establish its location in that area. Around the district of Nellore, there are villages like Kaṇṭepalle, Kaṭṭuvapalle and Kāṭepalle.[50] In the absence of clear evidences it is not easy to identify any one among them with 'Kaṭṭemu'.

Paṇḍaraṅga marched to Kandukur and embellished that city in commemoration of his victories, so as to make it look like Vijayavāḍa, the capital of the Eastern Chāḷukyas at that time. The burning of Nellore must have taken place on this occasion. He seems to have marched further south and annexed the territory extending upto the shore of the Pulikat lake. In the south of Nellore District, there is a village called Paṇḍaraṅgam with a shrine dedicated to the God Paṇḍaraṅgēśvara. That temple and village owe their origin obviously to this great Chāḷukyan general Paṇḍaraṅga, who founded them to commemorate his victory over the Bōyas.

In like manner, Paṇḍaraṅga undertook throughout his life so many expeditions against the Rāshṭrakūṭas and their allies, and was victorious. He destroyed and burnt Achalapura and Kiraṇa-pura ; captured Chakrakūṭa ; conquered Rāhaṇa, Sankila, Kannara, Mangi, Ḍāhala and Baddega. In the later inscriptions there was mention of Gaṅgas among the conquered. It was said that the expedition against the Gaṅgas and their conquest was done at the instance of Raṭṭēśa. Who this Raṭṭēśa was, and why Guṇaga Vijayāditya and Paṇḍaraṅga were obliged to carry out his word were not known. Whether Raṭṭēśa's word was a command or a request is utterly unknown. Possibly Raṭṭēśa could be identified with Rāshṭrakūṭa Kṛshṇa II. The word used in inscriptions in this connection is 'Saṁchōdita', i.e., 'challenged'.[51] Raṭṭēśa encouraged him to accomplish the task of overcoming Gaṅgas. N. Venkata Ramanayya condemned the meaning given to it and supplied it with another meaning 'commanded' or 'asked'.[52] But the probable Telugu word for 'Saṁchōdita' is 'prērēpiṁpabaḍi', i.e., being encouraged by or induced by ; and this meaning might convey the proper situation.

These successful military achievements of general Paṇḍaraṅga prompted the description of his as 'Bhībhatsu', 'the Terrible', (epic hero in prowess and valour) in one of his masters' inscriptions.[53]

Vikramakrānta śātravaḥ dvitīya yiva bhībhatsuh, pratāpavān

Maliyampūḍi inscription attributes the credit of all these victories of Guṇagavijayāditya to Kaṭakarāja Paṇḍaraṅga.[54]

Kiraṇapura madhakshīt kṛshṇarāja stitam yah tripura miva mahēśah paṇḍaraṅga pratāpī tadiha mukha sahasrai ranvita śyaśya śākyam gaṇana mamala kīrtī tasya sat sāhasānam

But Paṇḍaraṅga was modest enough to call himself the worshipper of the lotus feet of Guṇaga Vijayāditya (*Vijayāditya bhūpāla pāda padma śilīmukhah*).[55]

Paṇḍaraṅga's capital was Kandukur near the river Mannēru in the Nellore District. The territory over which he ruled as a feudatory of Guṇaga Vijayāditya must be presumably in the vicinity of Kandukur in the Nellore District and extended as far as Addanki taluq in the Prakasam District. He bore all the high titles of a great feudatory together with those of the commander-in-chief. Of his numerous exploits, the burning of Kiraṇapura especially was long remembered by his descendants even for four centuries after him.[56] Even though he was a parama-māhēśvara, he constructed a temple for Ādityabhaṭṭāraka, the Sun God, at Dhamavaram near Ongole and made several grants to it.

In the Sātalūru inscription of Guṇaga Vijayāditya, Paṇḍaraṅga was praised as *asidhārā samuchchhinna vidvadbṛndōpavanditah*[57] which means a person who was praised by the scholars whose heads were cut down. This is absurd. Divakarla Venkatavadhani noticed this as a fault and corrected as "*viḍvidbṛundōpavanditah*"[58] which means a person who was praised by scholars.

Paṇḍaraṅga's inscriptions are very important for Telugu literature as they furnish a positive proof that Telugu poetry was in evidence in the middle of the 9th century A.D. His Addanki inscription which contained Taruvōja type of stanzas, was the first of its kind in Telugu poetry. In his Kandukur pillar inscription there appeared a stanza of Sisa type of composition. In the Sātalūru inscription, for which he was also an executor, champakamāla type of verse could find place Even though this inscription was composed in Sanskrit, *prāsa,* which is not in common use among Sanskrit poets, was found in this. By this, some scholars presumed general Paṇḍaraṅga as the writer also of that grant.[59] If this presumption is correct, we can say that Paṇḍaraṅga is not only a famous commander on battle-fields, but also a scholar-poet in the realm of literature. He might be considered the first person to translate Sanskrit types of poems into Telugu, and we might call him as the first '*sāhitī samarāngaṇa sārvabhouma*' in the history of the Āndhras.

Starting with the Bōya campaign, Paṇḍaraṅga achieved successive victories in almost all the military campaigns of his master Guṇaga Vijayāditya. He was the outstanding hero of the age and his services to the Vēṅgī rulers remained a memorable record of achievements.

After Paṇḍaraṅga, his son Niravadyadhavaḷa occupied the hereditary office of his ancestor Kaṭakarāja, under Chāḷukya Bhīma I; but he died shortly afterwards. Then Chāḷukya Bhīma I appointed Vijayāditya, the son of Niravadyadhavaḷa to his hereditary office.[60] In addition to Vijayāditya, another by name Kaḍeyarāja II is reported in the records to be holding a similar office.[61] He was also a grandson of Paṇḍaraṅga. N. Venkata Ramanayya expressed the view that, in all probability,[62] both these persons were one and the same ; but his argument for this identification does not appear to be based on solid grounds.

Sarvalōkāśraya Vishṇuvardhana Chāḷukya Bhīma I granted a tax-free village named 'Mōga' to Śrīmahādēvī', the wife of Vijayāditya. It is said that the grant was made to her in grateful memory of the services rendered to him by her husband.[63]

The description in that inscription makes it clear that Śrīmahādēvī was very young and beautiful, and that she lost her husband in the service of the king ; and that in consideration of her sad plight she was gifted with this village of 'Mōga'. The executor of that grant was Kaṭakarāja II.

N. Venkataramanayya identified Kaṭakarāja II and Vijayāditya as one and the same. But by the Mōga grant we are sure that Kaṭakarāja II, the executor of that grant lived even after the death of Kaṭakādhipati Vijayāditya in whose memory the grant was made to Śrīmahādēvī. So there is no ground for this identification. Kaṭakarāja II and Kaṭakādhipati Vijayāditya were separate individuals in the same family, for Kaṭakarāja II also claimed his descent from Paṇḍaraṅga, according to the Nāgiyapūḍi grant of Amma II. We might regard Kaṭakarāja II as the brother of Vijayāditya, even though the relationship was not specifically mentioned.

The grant of the village 'Mōga' to Śrīmahādevī was only a token of gratitude for her husband's loyal services and the Chāḷukyan family did not cease to take interest but continued to extend favours to that family. Ammarāja II appointed Durgarāja, the son of Vijayāditya, as the Kaṭakādhipati. Next only to Paṇḍaraṅga in stature, Durgarāja seems to have been the powerful feudatory and talented commander-in-chief of this family. He was the "*Rāja-vishayādhyaksha*" in the province of Karmarāshṭra.[64]

It is proudly declared that he had the honour of being attended upon, on all ceremonial occasions and public functions, by the five great sounds and held the title 'mahāsāmanta'.[65] He was also described as an abode of virtues and righteousness, upholder of truth and justice, and one who knew the nobility of self-sacrifice. His sword was always kept unsheathed for the protection of the fortunes of the Chāḷukyas. His capital was Kandukur, the city which was remodelled by Paṇḍaraṅga, his great grand-father so as to equal the splendour of Vijayavāḍa. His kingdom lay apparently in the Kammanāḍu and extended to the river Svarṇamukhī in the south and to the river Guṇḍlakamma in the north thus comprising the whole of the Nellore District and the Ongole Taluq of the Prakasam District. A small seaport called "Durgarājapaṭnam' to the south of Svarṇamukhī seems to have been founded by this Durgarāja. He established a Jain temple at Dharmavaram in the Ongole Taluq and named it Kaṭakābharaṇa Jinālaya, evidently after his name. It is said that Amma II endowed the village of Maliyampūṇḍi in the Karmarāshṭra as a *dēvabhōga* to that Jain temple.[66] Durgarāja's minister was Mūsiyaśarman, a Brahmin of the Bhāradvāja *gōtra*. At the request of Durgarāja, Amma II granted a village 'Tumuyavēṇi', which has been classified as an agrahāra, to Mūsiyaśarman.[67]

Next to Durgarāja, one Paṇḍaraṅga II claimed his descent from Kaṭakarāja family. It seems, he was also in the royal service as a commander in the period of Amma II ; but for some unknown reasons, he gave up his allegiance and turned against his king and joined hands with Bādapa and the remaining chieftains, in a revolt against Amma II. We do not know in what measure he was rewarded for this help rendered to Bādapa ; probably he was made the supreme commander of the permanent hereditary forces. Bādapa in his Iṇṭēru grant referred to Paṇḍaraṅga as such.

Paṇḍaraṅgō yaśōnidhin, sūnuh kaṭakarājasya mūla vargaika nāyakah[68]

Durgarāja and Paṇḍaraṅga II were contemporaries. The former was the son of Kaṭakādhipati Vijayāditya and the latter was the son of Kaṭakarāja II. The genealogy of the family described in the Maliyaṁpūdi grant and other records may be amplified as follows :

- Bhaṭṭa Kāla
  - Kaḍeyarāja
    - Paṇḍaraṅga
      - Niravadyadhavaḷa
        - Vijayāditya
          - Durgarāja
        - Kaṭakarāja II
          - Paṇḍaraṅga II
    - Ayyapayya

After Durgarāja and Paṇḍaraṅga II, the succession in the family fell into obscurity. But evidence to the continuity of the rule of the Kaṭakarājas in the Vēṅgī kingdom was provided by a record. In the twelfth century, a Viceroy of the king of Vēṅgīmaṇḍala, a member of the Paṭṭavardhanīs, with the titles of 'kaḍeyarāya' and 'kiraṇapuradahanakara' ruled in the vicinity of Addanki.[69]

Another vassal family which ably assisted during the wars and in the administration of the Vēṅgī Chāḷukyan dominions was the Pānāra family. It is said that Pānāraṣ stood as a bulwark and offered protection to the Eastern Chāḷukyas. A well known commander in this family was Vajjiya. He served Chāḷukya Bhīma II and was praised as a treasure-house of truthfulness and valour. At the request of Vajjiya, Chāḷukya Bhīma II gave the village of koḍhatali in the kaṇḍēruvāṭivishaya, as an agrahāra to a Brahmin Kammana.[70]

Thus there were so many powerful feudatory families like Durjaya, Aryyahu, and Mitreyu, which continued in the royal service of the Eastern Chāḷukyas and some of which remained as faithful vassals of the kingdom till the days of complete disappearance of their sovereignty in Āndhradēśa.

REFERENCES

1. *E.I.*, Vol. XIX, p. 258.
2. *History of the Eastern Chāḷukyas of Vēṅgī*, p. 77.
3. *S.I.I.*, Vol. IV, No. 662.
4. *I.A.*, Vol. XIX, p. 15.
5. *I.A.*, Vol. XIII, p. 51 ; Vol. II, p. 175 ; *S.I.I.*, Vol. II, No. 25.
6. (i) *E.I.*, Vol. V, p. 139 ; *I.A.*, Vol. VIII, p. 74.
   (ii) *E.I.*, Vol. VII, p. 177.
7. *E.I.*, Vol. VII, p. 177.
8. *I.A.*, Vol. XIII, p. 51 ; Vol. II, p. 175 ; *S.I.I.*, Vol. II, No. 25.
9. *Ibid.*
10. *S.I.I.*, Vol. I No. 36.
11. *History of the Eastern Chāḷukyas of Vēṅgī*, p. 234.
12. *I.A.*, Vol. XIII, p. 51.
13. *Ibid.*, Vol. VIII, p. 74.
14. *History of the Eastern Chāḷukyas of Vēṅgī*, p. 280.
15. *I.A.*, Vol. XIII, p. 213.
16. *Ibid.*, p. 248.
17. *E.I.*, Vol. VII, p. 177.
18. *Ibid.*
19. *E.I.*, Vol. XIX, p. 137.
20. *I.A.*, Vol. XIII, p. 249.
21. *History of the Eastern Chāḷukyas of Vēṅgī*, p. 294.
22. *A.S.P.P.*, Vol. II, p. 241.
23. *I.A.*, Vol. VIII, p. 77 ; *E.I.*, Vol. V, p. 131.
24. *Ibid.*
25. *I.A.*, Vol. XIII, p. 50.

26. *Ibid.*, Vol. XX, p. 13.
27. *E.I.*, Vol. XIX, p. 271.
28. *Pallavulu-Chāḷukyulu*, p. 317.
29. *Bhārati*, Vol. I, Part I, p. 101 ; *J.A.H.R.S.*, Vol. V, p. 101.
30. *A.R.E.*, No. 3 of 1912-13, para No. 64 of 1913.
31. *E.I.*, Vol. V. p. 122.
32. *Epi. Āndhrica*, Vol. III, cp. No. 3.
33. *A.R.E.* cp. No. 3 of 1908-9, para 58 of 1909.
34. *Bhārati*, Vol. V, p. 619.
35. *Epi. Āndhrica*, Vol. III, cp. No. 5.
36. *E.I.*, Vol. IX, p. 47.
37. *J.A.H.R.S.*, Vol. XX, p. 195.
38. *The Eastern Chāḷukyas of Vēṅgī*, p. 131.
39. *History of the Eastern Chāḷukyas of Vēṅgī*, p. 188.
40. *Vēṅgī Chāḷukyulu*, p. 33.
41. *A.R.E.*, No. 106 of 1909.
42. *Pallavulu-Chāḷukyulu*, p. 345.
43. *Bhārati*, Vol. V, p. 619.
44. *E.I.*, Vol. XIX, p. 271.
45. *Epi. Āndhrica*, Vol. III, cp. No. 3.
46. *The Eastern Chāḷukyas of Vēṅgī*, *p*. 132.
47. *A.R.E.*, No. 27 of 1923.
48. *History of the Eastern Chāḷukyas of Vēṅgī*, p. 130.
49. *E.I.*, Vol. XIX, p. 271.
50. *Census Reports of Andhra Pradesh, Nellore District*, 1971.
51. *S.I.I.*, Vol. I, No. 36.
52. *The Eastern Chāḷukyas of Vēṅgī*, p. 103.
53. *E.I.*, Vol. V, p. 122.
54. *Ibid.*, Vol. IX, p. 47
55. *A.R.E.*, No. 3 of 1912-13, para 64.
56. *S.I.I.*, Vol. VI, No. 191.
57. *J.A.H.R.S.*, Vol. V, p. 101.

58. *Andhravañmayārambhadaśa*, Vol. I, p. 74.
59. *Telugu Kavula Charitra*, p. 25.
60. *E.I.*, Vol. V, p. 127.
61. *J.A.H.R.S.*, Vol. XX, p. 195.
62. *E.I.*, Vol. IX, p. 55.
63. *Epi. Āndhrica*, Vol. III, cp. No. 5.
64. *E.I.*, Vol. XVIII, p. 226.
65. *Ibid.*, Vol. IX, p. 45.
66. *E.I.*, Vol. IX, p. 47.
67. *Ibid.*, Vol. XVII, p. 274.
68. *A.R.E.*, No. 6 of 1938-39.
69. *S.I.I.*, Vol. VI, No. 191.
70. *Ibid.*, Vol. I, p. 46.

Jayasiṁha issued another grant[6] from Asanapura. This was addressed to the village of Kundūru in the Plaki-*vishaya*. He granted Kuḍivāḍa to the donees Svāmiyaśas and Vishṇuyaśas of the Vatsa *gōtra*, separating it from the boundary of Kundūru and constituting it into an agrahāra with all the usual immunities.

Similarly the first grant to the Pisṭapura plates of Jayasiṁha[7] was given from Asanapuravāsaka. The donee was Ādityaśarman, a brahmacharin of Gautama *gōtra* and a resident of Pisṭapura. The grant made is Mālekariyam a village which was situated in Pisṭapura-*vishaya*.

By the above mentioned sources we can know that Asanapura is an important Agrahāra flourishing then, where from a number of Brāhmaṇa scholars of various śāstras have hailed. Even though there is such frequent reference to this place in many inscriptions, the difficulty in identifying its locality is not a simple one. Asanapura is not a gifted village. It is the headquarters of the royal authority from where grants were issued. But we have not known the names of the boundary villages or the *vishaya* in which this Asanapura was located. In the above inscriptions it was just only mentioned as a residence of the donor or donee of both. This is the stage of its being unidentified even now by the historians and scholars. Whether it lay in the region of Visakhapatnam district or of the both Gōdāvarī districts or of Guntur District. It must be within the region of the four districts.

Firstly, we may say that 'Asana' might be the corrupt form of the word 'Āsana', otherwise known as 'pīṭha' (the seat). Then Asanapura may be identified with Piṭhāpuram, which the scholars like D.C. Sarkar and Ganguly, etc., think to be the first capital of the Eastern Chāḷukyas prior to Vēṅgī.[8] Prof. S.V. Joga Rao, basing on the first grant of Pisṭapura plates of Chāḷukya Jaysiṁha, by mistake mentioned that the king's residence was Pisṭapura.[9] So it is concluded that both Piṭhāpuram and Asanapura are identical. But this is liable to careful observation. Pisṭapura plates were given from Asanapura vasaka. It addressed the families of Piṭhāpuram. That shows Asanapura must have been separated. Moreover, there is no evidence literary or otherwise to tell that

Piṭhāpuram has another name like Asanapura. Piṭhāpuram was mentioned by that name only in the time of the Guptas, as known from Allahabad pillar inscription of Samudragupta mentioning 'Pisṭapuraka Mahēndra'. Therefore, to identify Asanapura with Piṭhāpuram may not be feasible.

Secondly, the term Asana is a prakrit form for 'Anna' which means 'meals'. This meaning suddenly takes us on to the place, the present Annavaram. Rao Bahadur Krishna Sastri is of the opinion that it is probably the ancient Asanapura. The adjacent Paṁpā waters and the surrounding agrahāras like Haṁsavaram etc., come to our aid to surmise that Annavaram also might be an agrahāra. So, Asanapura might be the present Annavaram. It may also be thought that Annavaram is so-called after the Reḍḍi kings in the latter period. This of course is subject to further proof.

Still another place like Āchellapurāgrahāra or Āchellapālem a village near Sarvasiddhi in the present Yellamanchili taluk, the then Plaki-*vishaya*, seems to answer our purpose. This is an agrahāra village having a hoary past as evidenced by numerous pottery remains and pāṭilands. Moreover, Jayasiṁha Vallabha, who issued all these grants had an epithet Sarvasiddhi. It is said that the present village Sarvasiddhi might have been constructed by this Jayasiṁha or by the later rulers in his name.[10] Sarvasiddhi is almost adjacent to this Āchellapurāgrahāra. So Sarvasiddhi Jayasiṁha might have constructed Sarvasiddhi, which name must have been given to Asanapura. We find instances in history that way as the present Delhi had been the seat of several dynasties under the name Hastināpura or Indraprasta or Shajahanabad of the times of Moghals; all in the neighbourhood of present Delhi. So Sarvasiddhi is quite close to Āchellapura. The locality of Āchellapuram and Sarvasiddhi may be taken to be the area comprising the ancient Asanapura. The earliest name might have been corrupted into Āchellapurāgrahāra, a hamlet now. If not he might have converted a part of Asanapura, as a royal residence giving a new name of Sarvasiddhi after his title. This method of formation of new villages and new towns or Agrahāras, re-arranging the boundaries seemed to have been the fancy of Jayasiṁha. There are other such examples like the one found in Ādivāsa grant. There he gifted the western portion of the village called Adivasa in Plaki-*vishaya* along with some of the fields of Kulivāṭaka, the present Guḍivāḍa near Sarvasiddhi, converting the whole area into an agrahāra.

Recently attempts are being made by some scholars[11] to consider Asanapura as the earliest name of 'Rājamahēndravara', the later capital of the Eastern Chāḷukyas.

Thus based upon mere etymological grounds in the absence of any other evidence so far many attempts have been made to identify Asanapura with various parts of Coastal Āndhra But none of them satisfactorily explains the later status of that village. Lack of epigraphical reference to any of these villages multiplies the doubt regarding their identification with Asanapura.

If Asanapura occupies so much importance, we have to seek the reason for its disappearance from inscriptions after Jayasiṁha. No ruler of this lineage after him mentioned about this. But, one ruler Vishṇuvardhana II, in his Pallevāḍa grant mentioned Asanapura as the earliest residence of the grand-father of his donee, Dhruvaśarman. Why its mention is not found later should be known. The political condition at the time was such that there was complete chaos and confusion, not only on account of neighbouring invasions but also of mutual rivalries between the dynasties of the then Āndhradēśa.[12] Nothing is known about the events of Jayasiṁha's reign period. It is known from the Pulimburu grant and Pisṭapura IInd grant, which were issued from his Vijayaskandhāvāras, his reign was not entirely peaceful. Who the enemies were and what the circumstances in which Jayasiṁhavallabha had to fight were utterly unknown.

N. Venkata Ramanayya also pointed out[13] that the date of accession of Jayasiṁhavallabha coincided with the date of destruction of Vātāpī and the temporary subversion of the Western Chāḷukyan monarchy. Narasiṁhavarman I, in all likelihood, made an attempt to recover the territory wrested from him earlier by Pulakēśin II. This means to say the position of the king Jayasiṁha was not at all stable and safe. In one of those ravages, by local chieftains Asanapura might have suffered the same fate as

Vātāpī. Destruction of enemy towns and capitals was a common feature with the kings then. Jayasiṁha too was no exception.

As such was the fate of Chāḷukyan agrahāras in the later period, we have to study the details of all the ancient agrahāra sites particularly in the Godavary valley for the identification of Asanapura. The inscriptions of Drākshārāma help us in this matter. One damaged inscription[14] of the twelfth century, dated in the 26th regnal year (of Kulōttunga Chōḷa III) found there gives clue about this ancient village. In that inscription Asanapura is mentioned as Ḥasanapura; and this eeems to be the last epigraphical reference to Asanapura. If we consider Hasanpura as the changed form of ancient Asanapura, there is every possibility to identify it with the present 'Hasanabada', a small village near Drākshārāma. Though Hasanabada and its surroundings did not yield any archaeological evidences, in view of the importance as well as antiquity of the locality around Drākshārāma in the period of the Chāḷukyas, we may identify Hasanabada as the acient Asanapura, which had a hoary past in the Chāḷukyan period.

TEXT OF THE CHĀḶUKYAN INSCRIPTION WHICH REFERS TO ASANAPURA IN THE TWELFTH CENTURY

1. ... ...
2. Saṁvatsa 26(gu) śrāhi Śrī Bhīmēśvara mahādēvaraku uttarāyaṇa Sankrānti nimittamuna
3. *Hasanapurapu* māvanabhaṭla penḍla (mu ve) lla mūri dēvana Appana talli muttanamma tanaku dha-
4. ṛmārdhamuṁ gā bōlu naluvura pūṇṭaga mahēśvara yeṛya bhōni vaśamunam beṭṭina ara.
5. divya/ṇṭi ki Inupayeḍlu 25 (/*) ā chandrārkamu nitya paḍi vōyam gala Tribhuvanāṁku
6. śa nē tavya/nit likitam peddanāchāri (sū) rāchārya (//*)

REFERENCES

1. *Indian Antiquity*, Vol. VII, p.191.
2. (i) *Epigraphia Indica*, Vol. XVIII, p. 137.
   (ii) *Ibid.*, Vol. XIX, p. 254.
   (iii) *Ibid.*, Vol. XXXI, p. 134.
   (iv) *Ibid.*, Vol. XXXI, p. 136.
   (v) *Bhārati*, 1963, December, p. 19.
3. *Indian Antiquity*, Vol. XX, p. 97.
4. *Journal of Andhra Historical Research Society*, Vol. IV, p. 72.
5. *Epigraphia Indica*, Vol. XXXI, p. 134.
6. *Ibid.*, p. 136.
7. *Bhārati*, 1963, December, p. 19.
8. *The Successors of Satavahanas*, p. 117.
9. *Bhārati*, 1963, December, p. 19.
10. *Samagra Āndhra Sāhityam*, Vol. IV, p. 98.
11. *Bhārati*, 1982, May, p. 50.
12. *The Eastern Chāḷukyas of Vēṅgī*, p. 64.
13. *Ibid.*
14. *South Indian Inscriptions*, Vol. IV, No. 1219.

3

THE EARLIEST RECORD OF THE CHĀḶUKYAS OF VĒMULAVĀḌA

One of the most important minor Chāḷukya branches that ruled over parts of the present Telangāṇa in the eighth, ninth and tenth centuries, and the one which played a prominent part in the political set-up of the period in the Deccan, is the Chāḷukya branch at Vēmulavāḍa. Two copper plate grants i.e., the Kollipaṛa plates of Arikēsari I[1] and the Parabhanī plates of Arikēsari III[2], lithic records at places like Kuravagaṭṭa[3] (Mahaboobnagar District), Vēmulavāḍa,[4] Karimnagar[5] and Rēpāka[6] (Karimnagar District); and the two literary works written under their patronage *Vikramārjuna Vijaya* by Paṁpa, and *Yaśastilaka* by Sōmadēvasūri form the main source of information regarding the history of this family. On the basis of the information provided by these sources, previously N. Venkataramanayya[7] constructed the genealogy of this family in the following way :

- Vinayāditya-Yuddhamalla
  - Arikēsari I
    - Narasiṁha I
      - Yuddhamalla II
        - Baddega
          - Yuddhamalla III
            - Narasiṁha II
              - Arikēsari II
                - Vāgarāja
                - Bhadradēva
                  - Arikēsari III
    - Bhadradēva
  - Vīragṛh

But in this genealogical scheme N. Venkataramanayya did not utilise the information known from the Kollipaṛa plates. He suspected the genuineness of that grant and concluded that Vinayāditya-Yuddhamalla, the father of Arikēsari I is the early known ruler in this family. The aim of this paper is to study about the genuineness of those Kollipaṛa plates.

The Kollipaṛa plates, the earliest of the inscriptions of this family, register the grant (*Vidyādāna*) by king Arikēsari I, son of Vinayāditya-Yuddhamalla of the Chāḷukya family to Mugdhaśivāchārya, a disciple of Sadyaśśivāchārya of the Ankuṭa-gurukula of the village of Belmoga in Rāmaḍuvishaya. It narrates the six generations of this family as Satyāśraya, Pṛthivīpati, Mahārāja, Rājāditya, Vinayāditya-Yuddhamalla and Arikēsari successively.

Vinayāditya-Yuddhamalla, the father of the donor king Arikēsari is stated to have been a great conqueror and was served by the kings of several countries such as Turushka, Yavana, Barbara, Kāśmīra, Kāṁbhōja, Magadha, Māḷava, Kaḷiṅga, Gaṅga, Pallava, Pāṇḍya and Kēraḷa. The script used in this inscription is the Telugu-Kannaḍa script of the Middle variety, that was in use in the Deccan from 8th to 10th century A.D. Even though this inscription mentions the earlist rulers of this family, their connections or relations with the other contemporary powers are not clear. The donor of this grant Arikēsari I is referred to in *Vikramārjuna Vijayam* as a contemporary of the Rāshṭrakuṭa king Nirupama Dhruva who ruled in between A.D. 780 and 793. Hence the grant mentioned in the Kollipaṛa plates might have also belonged to the same period ; and the paleography supports the above date. So the Kollipaṛa plates can be taken as a reliable grant given by Arikēsari I.

N. Venkataramanayya dubbed the political information mentioned in those plates as mythical. The following two are his main objections to accepting the genuineness of this record.[8]

(*i*) Inscriptions of a later period and *Vikramārjuna-vijayam* trace the descent of the family from Vinayāditya-Yuddhamalla. In them he is said to have ruled over the Sapādalaksha country, a country that could be governed by others ; that he has caused all his elephants to be bathed in a reservoir filled with oil at Pōdana ; and that he has captured a fort called Chitrakūṭa which was inaccessible. His son, Arikēsari I, is said to have conquered the kingdom of Vēṅgi and Trikaḷiṅga during the time of Nirupama Dhruva, the Rāshṭrakūṭa king who ruled from A.D. 780 to 793. These achievements are not mentioned in the Kollipaṛa plates, even though the same Arikēsari I, son of Vinayāditya-Yuddhamalla, issued those plates. While describing his father, he just mentioned about his conquests of Turushka, Yavana, Barbara, Kāśmīra, Kāṁbhōja, Magadha, Māḷava, Kaḷiṅga, Gaṅga, Pallava, Pāṇḍya and Kēraḷa.

(*ii*) Various researches done by scholars like M. Somasekhara Sarma and Muliya Timmappayya have not yielded good results ; and they cannot be considered successful in identifying the early rulers of this branch, known through these Kollipaṛa plates, with the Chāḷukya branches of Badami and Lāṭa. From this, it may be said that the genealogy given in the Kollipaṛa plates is a fictitious one. These chiefs probably forgot their real line of descent and fabricated the names of Satyāśraya-Raṇavikrama, Pṛthivīpati, Mahārāja and Rājāditya to reinforce their claim for rulership. Under this impression, N. Venkataramanayya rejected "not only the genealogy but also the history" mentioned in these Kollipaṛa plates.

But the objections raised by him against the genuineness of this grant do not appear convincing. He does not reject the fact of the issue of the grant by Arikēsari I. He expressed a doubt as to why the details mentioned in literature are absent in the inscription. He points out that Kollipaṛa plates did not mention some important achievements of Vinayāditya-Yuddhamalla I and Arikēsari I. The cause for this omission is not known. This omission does not undermine the genuineness of the grant ; it only makes the record incomplete or imperfect. Not only in this grant but also in the parabhanī plates, the capture of the fort Chitrakūṭa by Vinayāditya-Yuddhamalla is omitted. Could this omission make that grant also suspect about the genuineness ? The Karimnagar pillar inscription of Arikēsari III referred only to five generations even though he had full knowledge of his *entire* ancestry. For some reason or other, some sources may have omitted some facts. In the present context, Arikēsari I's conquest of Vēṅgī and Trikaḷiṅga might have occurred after the date of issue of this grant and hence they might not have been included in it. Similar might be the case with his father's achievements. As he added a list of countries conquered by his father, he might not have made a special mention of the conquest of Chitrakūṭa, which formed a part of the above-said countries. His successors of a later date left all other details and selected only some important conquests among which the conquest of Chitrakūṭa was the foremost.

Hence the first objection of N. Venkataramanayya to the genuineness of Kollipaṛa plates on the slender plea of their non-mention of details of all the achievements of the donor and his father cannot be regarded as well-founded.

The second point of doubt is about the relation and identity of these early rulers with the contemporary rulers of the other Chāḷukya families. As this genealogy in the Kollipaṛa plates begins with Satyāśraya-Raṇavikrama, some scholars identified him with Pulikēśi I,[9] the founder of the Chāḷukya dynasty of Bādāmī who ruled from A.D. 543 to 566. But this Satyāśraya-Raṇavikrama is five generations earlier to Arikēsari I, who lived in the time of Rāshṭrakūṭa Nirupama Dhruva who ruled from A.D. 780 to 793. On the basis of this, by allotting 25 years for each generation, we get A.D. 655 as the probable date of commencement of the rule of this Satyāśraya. As such, there is no warrant to identify him with Satyāśraya of the Bādāmī line who was a century ahead of him.

Basing on the similarity of the names of these early rulers with the epithets of the rulers of the Bādāmī family, scholars like Mallampalli Somasekhara Sarma and Muliya Timmappyya attempted to identify them with the rulers of the Bādāmī family.[10] But finding that such an identification was replete with problems, Somasekhara Sarma came to the conclusion that there was no scope to identify these rulers with the Bādāmī family. But, unlike him, Timmappayya went a little further and identified this Vinayāditya-Yuddhamalla with one Vinayāditya-Yuddhamalla of the Lāṭa branch of the Chāḷukyas. But as he himself pointed out, that there was no correspondence in their father's names. The names of the father of Vinayāditya-Yuddhamalla of the Lāṭa branch was Jayasiṁha, whereas the father of Vinayāditya-Yuddhamalla of Kollipaṛa plates was Rajāditya-Pṛthuvikrama. It does not seem justifiable to think that the same Jayasiṁha of the Lāṭa branch had "Rājāditya" and "Pṛthuvikrama" as his epithets in these Kollipaṛa plates, as it is not supported by other evidences. The inscriptions of Jayasiṁha of the Lāṭa branch and of his successors nowhere mentioned titles like "Rājāditya" and

"Pṛthuvikrama" for Jayasiṁha. Moreover, the actual name of his son Vinayāditya-Yuddhamalla is Mangalarasarāja, which is not applicable to the case of this Vinayāditya-Yuddhamala of the Kollipaṛa plates. Hence, it does not seem proper to accept this identification of Vinayāditya-Yuddhamalla with Mangalarasarāja, even though they belonged to the self same period. Venkataramanayya also refuted this identity and stated that this Vēmulavāḍa branch had no relations or connections with the Lāṭa branch.[11] All this goes to prove that the Vēmulavāḍa Chāḷukya branch was distinct and its early ruler Satyāśraya need not be identified with Satyāśraya Pulikēśi I, who lived a century before him.

Bhavaraju Venkata Krishna Rao states that Āditya Varma, a son of Pulikēśi II was the founder of this line.[12] Basing on the coincidence of time, one may assume that Satyāśraya Pulikēśi Vallabha II was the founder of this line. But the genealogical differences make us believe this Satyāśraya is a different king. So this branch may have had its own ancestry ; and its authenticity need not be rejected unless strong evidence of considerable contradiction emerges. It may therefore be safely assumed that there are six generations of rulers as stated in the Kollipaṛa plates who are the earliest members of the Chāḷukya family of Vēmulavāḍa.

TEXT OF THE INSCRIPTION
FIRST PLATE—SECOND SIDE

1. Om (//*) Jayaty=amala-jānhavī-jala-taraṁga saṁghāta-bhri (/*) jjaṭā makuṭa-
2. Vishphu (sphu) rat=taruṇa-Chandra-chūḍāmaṇi (ḥ/*) . . . . yapushā-jena-vapu (?) sha
3. vapur=manōhara-tara . . . . ḥ// (1/*)
4. Vyābhug=vaprō . . . . śrī . . . . gra . . . śa (/*) ghōṇ=ā
5. ghāt=ābhighāta-pa . . . . . la-śaila-prata-(?) dhvāna . . . . dai
6. tya=pramudita-vidi-vikrama=ākrānta-nā pāyād=ā . . . . . . kuvalaya.
7. vyāpinaś=chkrapāṇiḥ // (2*) . . . . ndara-śikhara-śilā-ghṛshṭi-dō

SECOND PLATE—FIRST SIDE

8. shō-jit=ārai (/*) prōd=bhindan=nābhi-padmā=āś-rīta-kamala-bhuvaś=chakriṇaḥ krōḍa-rūpa(ṁ ?)

9. bhūtam=bhūtyai = bhuvō-yad = dhṛita-sakala-dharā-maṇḍalam tat=prasāda-prādur=bhūtō dharā-ra-

10. kshaṇa-paṭur=amalaś=chāru-Chāḷukya-vaṁśaḥ // (3*) Tasmin=vaṁśē kalābhṛit-kala-ka-

11. li-janita-dhvānta-bhit=saumya vṛittiḥ (/*) kshīr=ōdanvaty=udaṁśuś uś=śaśa-dhara iva yaḥ prā-

12. dūr=āsīn=mahātmā(/*)Utkhāt=āsī-pratāpāv=anamita-ripubhūbhṛit=Kulō bhūta-daitryā (/*)

13. bharttā Satyāśrayas=sa-prabhu-guṇa-mahitō bhūtala-khyāta-kīrtti (ḥ*) Ēstasmād=Ra-

14. ṇa-Vikramāt = pṛithu-balāt = Satyāśraya-kshmā-bhṛi-taḥ (/*) pṛithvīśah Pṛithvīpati (ḥ*) Pṛthu-nibhō

15. lōka-stutō = bhūt=sutaḥ (/*) tasmāt=tat = Prithivī-patēr=vvasumatī-khyātō Mahārāja-

16. (? kaḥ) (/*) (tyā) (g=audā*) (ryya-) varaḥ (pa*) (rā)-ritha-(nira) taḥ prādū (r = bba) = bhūv = ātmajah// (5*) Āsīt = tasmā (n=ma) (hā*) rājā (d = ā-)

17. tmaja(ḥ*) pṛithu-vikramaḥ (/*) Pṛithu-Māndhātṛi-saṁ-kāśō Rājādityō dharādhipati (//6*) Tatō = bhavat=suta (ḥ*) śrī-

18. mān Śrīrāmō Rāma-vikramaḥ (/*) viśvarāḍ = Vinayā-dityō Yuddhamallō nṛip = āṁkuśaḥ // (7*)

19. Guru-dōr =ddaṇḍa-prachaṇḍasphurad=asi-latik=ānīta-rājanya-lakshmī (/*) kara-yugm=ōtthā-

20. pit-ēndu-dyuti-hara-dhavaḷ = āmbhōja-līl = ātapatraḥ (/*) dharaṇī-dik=chakravāḷ=āntaga-nikhi-

21. la-guṇ = ōdbhāsi rāj = āśrayas sā (/*) gara-vēlā-vēsh-ṭit=ōdyat=sakala-vasumatī-vallabhō

22. Yuddhamallaḥ // (8*) Turushka-Yavana-Barbara-Kāsmīra-Kāmbhōja - Magadha - Māḷava - Kaḷiṁga-Gaṁga (ga)
23. Pallava - Pāṇḍya - Kēraḷa - prabhṛiti - narapati - sa-saṁbhrama samarppita-pāda-pīṭaḥ

THIRD PLATE—FIRST SIDE

24. Bhagavan= Nārāyaṇa-vara-varaha - lāñchchana-vaśīkrat aśēsha-viśvāmbharā-chakraḥ//
25. Abhavad=Vinayādityān=Nala (Na) (husha-Di*) (lī) pa-Dundhumāra-pratimān (/*) Arikēsar=iti
26. nāmnā sūnuḥ kshīr = ōdādhēr-yaḍā śiśr = āṁśuḥ (//9*) Rāja-śrīyaṁ vakshasi bhāratīm=mukhē vīra-
27. śrīyan = dōshi gurau sva-dakshiṇē (/*) dik-chakra-vāḷa-bhıamaṇ=ōdyatān=dadhat (/*) kīrtti-
28. pratāpē ripu-darppa-nāsanē (// 10*) Vyākaraṇa-tharmma-vid=dvirada-tantra-daksha (s*) = sadā
29. nyāya-nipuṇo dhanur = vvidita-śikshayā-viśrutaḥ āyatim=upētavān=jagati vaidya-śā
30. stro=ḍhikām śrīmad = Arikēsarī nṛipa-guṇais-sam=āvishkrataḥ (//11*) samastha bhuvana-raja
31. (?la*) kshmī-nivāsa-(stha) laḥ sva-bhuja-bal=akraṣhṭa-śar=āsana-jyā-latā.
32. vimu (kta) nārācha-paramparā-parājita - par-āvanipāla saṁ=stūyamāna raṇ=Ārjunaḥ
33. śumbhadh = ambhōdhī-mēkhalā-kalāp = āvṛita-vasundharā-tala-sandhāraṇa sthambhāya-
34. māna bhuj=ārggaḷah samastha-lōkāśrayah tribhu-vana-mallaḥ-rāja-triṇētraḥ sā-
35. hasa-rāmaḥ ity=ētair=abhidhānair=abhishṭutaḥ (//*) Kalō vyāptē jagaty=asmin=surēndrō-

36. bhārkka-sāgarāḥ (/*) dānēna tējasē sthityā jitā yēna mahātmanaḥ (//12*) Aṁkkuṭa-gu-

37. ru-kulēna Śaiv=āchāryyair = avāpta-tapaḥ-prabhāvā-sya Śrīkanṭh=āvāsa-Śrīparvvat=ō

38. ttara-dvārē paschād=Elīsvarē krata-nilayē sadā=sāk aharinaṁ Sa (dya)-śiv=āchāryya-

39. sya śishyah (//*) siddhānta-baddha-buddhi(ḥ*) dhyā-na-pradhvasth-durita-praba (ndha)-prachaya (ḥ*)

40. mugdha-śaśi - śēkhara Śrī Mugdha - śivō - nāma-śuddha-charitō mahitaḥ (//13*) tasmai mahāmunayē

41. Śrīmad = Arikēsariṇa samastha-lōkāsrayēna rājā-triṇē-trēṇa (//*) (pūrvv=ō) ditē (na*) kshiti-

42. bhṛit = sutēna rāj=āṁkuśēn = āhava - vikramēṇa (/*) grāmaś = Siv - ārādhana-tat=par - ārttaṁ tapasvi-

43. nē Mugdha - śivāya dattaḥ (// 14*) Ayaṁ śrīmad=Ari-kēsa (ri*) ṇo dharmmaḥ (//*) Vidyā-dānam=idam

44. datta (ṁ) m (//*) Sa grāmaḥ Rāmaḍu-Vishē Ūrige-nāmū-vikhyāta-mahā-grāmasya-dakshi-

45. ṇa-dig = bhāga-sthitō grāmaḥ Belomogam = iti nāmnā viśrutaḥ Tuvatoru parivaturla (?)

46. Pul=cheṛuvuḷ pōtuvōdupi ity=ētēshām grāmaṇām sa madhya sthitaḥ (/*)

47. Utkam cha Manv-=ādibhiḥ (//*) Sva-dattaṁ para-dattaṁ va yō hārēta vasuōdharā (/*) shashiṭīm va-

48. raha-sahasrāni vishṭāyāṁ jāyatē krimiḥ (//15//*) Bhūmi-dānāt=paraṁ puṇyam nabhū-

49. tō na bhavishyati (/*) tasyai vakrāt=paraṁ pāpō na bhūtō na bhavishyati (//16*) Bahu-

50. bhir = vvasudhāṁ bhuktō rājabhis = Sagar = ādibhiḥ (/*) yasya (yasya*) yathā bhūmis=tasya

51. tasya tadā phalaṁ (// 17* //) Triṇ = āgra - viśrānta-tushāra-sañchalaṁ śriyan = tatha jī-

52. vitam = ātmanaḥ pumān (/*) sam = ikshya buddhyā dvija-dēva-dattīshu pralōbhyēt=kaṛ=para

REFERENCES

1. *Bhārati*, August, 1930, pp. 297-318.
2. *The Chāḷukyas of L(V)ēmulavāḍa*, p. 92.
3. *Kannada Inscriptions of Andhra Pradesh*, No 29.
4. *Inscriptions of Andhra Pradesh*, Karimnager District, No. 2
5. *Ibid*., No. 1.
6. *Ibid*., No. 5.
7. *The Chāḷukyas of L(V)ēmulavāḍa*, p. 9.
8. *Ibid*., pp.7-8.
9. *Bhārati*, August, 1930, pp. 297-318.
10. *Ibid*.
11. *Pallavulu-Chāḷukyulu*, p.161.
12. *History of the Eastern Chāḷukyas of Vēṅgī*, p. 153.

4

A CRITICAL TELUGU INSCRIPTION OF THE VIRIYĀLAS

One of the most important inscriptions in Eastern Telaṅgāṇa, which mentions the unique political event that relates to three subordinate families—Viriyālas, Kākatīyas and Mudigoṇḍa Chāḷukyas, is the Gudur inscription of Viriyāla Malla.[1] This was written on one face of the pillar consisting of five Telugu vṛtta stanzas, which praise the exploits of the ancestors of Viriyāla Malla. This is undated, but might belong to the period of Tribhuvanamalla Vikramāditya VI, of the Kalyāṇī Chāḷukyā family. The remaining three faces of the pillar have an inscription of Kumāra Sōmēśvara (son of Vikramāditya VI) which tells us of his grants to the temple of Śiva, named Mallēśvara, which was constructed by this Viriyāla Malla in Guṁḍūru.[2] This gift was made in the 49th year of the Chāḷukya Vikrama era which corresponds to A.D. 1124. This date is given for Malla's inscription also owing to the proximity of both the inscriptions as well as the identity of the engravers of both the inscriprions.

The timing of the historical events, the uncertain meaning for some terms used in this inscription, and the lack of interconnection among these five stanzas necessitated a good discussion among scholars.

Dr. P. Srinivasachar,[3] Sri K. Harshavardhana Sarma,[4] Sri Chilukuri Papayya Sastri,[5] Sri Tekumalla Kameswara Rao,[6] Sri Vedam Venkataraya Sastri,[7] Sri Bhagavatula Lakshminarayana,[8] and lastly Dr. P.V. Parabrahma Sastry[9] contributed to be discussion, and threw light on the history of the period. This much is done in the last two decades. With the re-editing of the Kṛivvaka grant of Kusumāditya of the Mudigoṇḍa Chalukyan family by Dr. Parabrahmma Sastry,[10] the hitherto unknown history of this Mudigoṇḍa family came to light and to some extent it helped in revealing the meaning of this Gudur inscription.

Among these five stanzas, the third and the fourth are very important as they narrate the exploits of Viriyāla Eṛṛa and his wife Kāmsānī. In that context it is mentioned that Eṛṛanṛipa, the ancestor of this Viriyāla Malla killed the enemies of Boṭṭu Bēta must be one among the family of the Mudigoṇḍa Chāḷukyas, as the rulers of the same name were found in the later inscriptions of that family.[11] The historical significance of the Gudur inscription lies in the role played by the Viriyāla couple, Eṛṛa and Kāmasānī. Both have championed different political issues connected with two Bētas, who are referred to in this inscription. They are Boṭṭu Bēta and Kākati Bēta. In the first context Eṛṛa initiated and guided the cause of Boṭṭu Bēta, conquerred his enemies and reinstated him in the Koravi kingdom. As a reward for this help he was given some villages like that of Mogaḍupalli. The place of the battle and the identity of his enemies are not known. Because at this time Eastern Telaṅgāṇa was in unsettled political condition, it is not easy to estimate what has actually happened. The respective dates of inscriptions found in these areas do not help us to know the correct position. But it is known that all the three families—Viriyālas, Kākatīyas and the Chāḷukyas of Mudigoṇḍa, were only having subordinate status. At one time or other all of them accepted the suzerainty of the Chāḷukyas of Kalyāṇī. Because the king of Kalyāṇī did not participate in any of the wars mentioned in this Gudur inscription, we can say that these were the disputes among local rulers. The available evidence does not lead to the identification of the enemy of this Boṭṭu Bēta of the Mudigoṇḍa family. He might be a prince of Kākatīya or non-Kākatīya family. This much is mentioned about Boṭṭu Bēta in this inscription. Another Bēta, i.e., Kākati Bēta on whose side Kāmasānī championed and helped for the resettlement of the Kākatīyas, is also referred to in this inscription.

Thus altogether two Bētarājas, one being the Mudigoṇḍa Chāḷukya and the other the Kākatīya are mentioned in this inscription. Now, the object of this article is to identify who were both these Bētarājas and what was their place in their respective dynasties.

Boṭṭu Bēta of the Mudigoṇḍa Chāḷukyan family was helped by Viṛlyāla Eṟṟa in one context, whereas Kākati Bēta was saved by Kāmasānī, the wife of this Viriyāla Eṟṟa, on another occasion. So one can accept that both these Bētas were contemporaneous at least for a short period, because they were helped by Viriyāla couple. Thus they should have lived in the same period, and the chronology of these three families, i.e., the Chāḷukyas of Mudigoṇḍa, the Viriyālas and the Kākatīyas can only help us to identify both these Bētas. Without chronological basis the problem cannot be solved. So before identifying these kings our first requisite is to study the chronology of these families.

Firstly, let us take the chronology of the Chāḷukyas of Mudigoṇḍa. Even though Dr. Parabrahmma Sastry tried to give a complete picture of the genealogy of the family, in the recent issues of *Bhārati* he has not dealt with the chronology in detail and has identified kings known from different inscriptions with kings known from Mogalicheruvula and Kṛivvaka grants arbitrarily.[12] Because there is no concrete evidence to fix the definite periods of the early rulers of the family, we have calculated from the known dates of the later rulers of the same family. Except this there is no other method to reconstruct the chronology of the Chāḷukyas of Mudigoṇḍa.

As the evidence of paleography suggests, Kṛivvaka grant of Chāḷukya Kusumāditya belongs to the 12th Century. In that inscription the last mentioned rulers were two brothers, named Kusumāditya and Nāgatirāja. The same Nāgatirāja was again referred to in the Palampet inscription[13] of Rēcherla Rudra of A.D. 1213 and in the Nattarāmēśvaram inscription[14] of Kolanu chiefs in A.D. 1218. With the help of these two inscriptions it is possible to fix the date of Nāgati, the last ruler mentioned in the Kṛivvaka grant to be A.D. 1200. Taking this year as a basis, by allowing 25 years of rule to each generation, the eight rulers in the Kṛivvaka grant should be dated to A.D. 1000-1200. By this method of allotment, Nāgati ruled in A.D. 1200 ; Goṇaga or Kariya Goṇaga was a ruler in between A.D. 1000-1025, as supported by Nārāyaṇagiri inscription[15] of A.D. 1004; and Kusumāyudha IV was ruling in between A.D. 1050-1075 as supported by the date assigned to the Mogalicheruvula grant by the Prof. Bendall basing on paleography. Dr. Parabrahmma Sastry opines that the Goṇagas mentioned in the Kṛivvka grant and Koravi inscription[16] are one and the same ; and with that assumption prepared the genealogy of this family. But this Goṇaga of Kṛivvka grant should not be identified with that Koravi Goṇaga as there is much difference in their times. Koravi Goṇaga ruled from A.D. 895 whereas Goṇaga of Kṛivvaka grant ruled in between A.D. 1000-1025. Chronology permits us to identify Kariya Goṇaga with the Goṇaga of Nārāyaṇagiri inscription only. Thus the fixing of the eight rulers mentioned in the Kṛivvaka grant in between A.D. 1000 and A.D. 1200, is justified.

Next let us fix the periods of the early rulers of this family. Kusumāyudha I, Bijayita Goṇaga, and Niravadya are three early rulers mentioned in the Koravi inscription. These three were contemporaries of Chāḷukya Bhīma I (A.D. 892-922) at least for a short period. Chāḷukya Bhīma I in his early stages was helped in wars by this Kusumāyudha and at his request only Chāḷukya Bhīma I granted Kūkipaṟṟu to a brahmin as mentioned in Bezwada plates.[17] A short period after the coronation of Chāḷukya Bhīma I, this Kusumāyudha might have died and Bijayita Goṇaga became king as noted in the Koravi epigraph. But it seems he was not allowed to rule for a long period by Niravadya who dethroned him and occupied the throne. At this time the Vēṅgī Chāḷukyan government was in the midst of problems like internecinde wars and wars with the Rāshṭrakūṭas. We do not know the understanding between Chāḷukya Bhīma I and Niravadya in ousting Bijayita Goṇaga. Only because his was an usurpation, it probably became necessary for Peddana to seek confirmation of the rights in collecting taxes, etc., from Niravadya, as mentioned in Koravi epigraph. By this time Bijayita Goṇaga did not die as some historians suggested.[18] He could not challenge his brother as his relations with Rāshṭrakūtas and Vēṅgi Chāḷukyas were not cordial. Hence he had to seek shelter in the court of his neighbour, another Chalukyan prince of Vēmulavāḍa i.e., Arikēsari II. His protection by Arikēsari II is mentioned in the *Vikramārjunavijayam* of Paṁpa, and in the Vēmulavāḍa inscription of Arikēsari.[19] Later this Goṇaga's son Baddega served Arikēsari II as a subordinate, as known from Chennur epigraph.[20] Thus basing on the contemporary political scene and on the inscriptions at Koravi and Chennur, we can fix the rule of these three rulers of the Koravi epigraph as follows—Kusumāyudha I A.D. 870-895; Bijayita Goṇaga A.D. 895-910 ; and Niravadya A.D. 910-935. Only Kusumāyudha I and Niravadya were allotted 25 years rule. Bijayita Goṇaga, as he was not allowed to rule for complete period, was allotted only 15 years rule even though he lived for 20 years more, i.e., upto A.D. 935 in the court of Arikēsari II.

Thus the first set of three rulers mentioned in Koravi epigraph are fixed in between A.D. 870 and A.D. 935 ; and the last set of eight rulers mentioned in the Kṛivvaka grant are fixed in between A.D. 1000 and A.D. 1200. In the mean period, between the two sets of rulers as inscriptions suggest, there are three rulers Kusumāyudha II, Vijayāditya and Kusumāyudha III. These three rulers had to share the remaining period of 65 years (between A.D. 935 and A.D. 1000). Then finally the geneological and chronological table of the Mudigoṇḍa Chāḷukyan family can be formuloted as follows :

- ?
  - Kokkirāja
  - Raṇamarda
    - Kusumāyudha I (A.D. 870-895)
      - Goṇaga or Vijayāditya (A.D. 895-910)
        - Baddega (A.D. 935-941)
        - Kusumāyudha II (A.D. 935-960)
          - Vijayāditya (A.D. 960-980)
            - Kusumāyudha III (A.D. 980-1000)
              - Goṇaga (A.D. 1000-1025)
              - Nijjayarāja (A.D. 1025-1050)
                - Kusumāyudha IV (A.D. 1050-1075)
                  - Bētarāja (A.D. 1075-1100)
                    - Kusumāyudha V (A.D. 1100-1125)
                      - Boṭṭu Bēta (A.D. 1125-1150)
                        - Kusumāditya or Kusumāyudha VI (A.D. 1150-1175)
                        - Nāgatirāja (A.D. 1175-1200)
              - Mallapa
              - Lōbhachḷaka
      - Niravadya (A.D. 910-935)

The limitation in fixing the chronology are—

(*i*) Mallapa and Lōbhachaḷaka are not taken as rulers as they are mentioned nowhere as kings.

(*ii*) Absence of reference to Niravadya and Kariya Goṇaga in some inscriptions is taken to have happened due to the rivalry or due to any other similar cause.

(*iii*) Finally, Malliya and Guṇḍiya referred to in the Kaṇḍyam plates of Dānārṇava are not considered as rulers as their migration to Pottāpināḍu is evident : and they are not associated with this main family.

Subject to these limitations, we have arranged the chronology of these 14 rulers of the Mudigoṇḍa Chāḷukyan family, in between A.D. 870 and A.D. 1200.

The next chronology is that of the Viriyālas which helps in solving the present problem. As mentioned already these Viriyālas were a māṇḍalika family, which ruled in the districts of Telaṅgāṇa in the 11th, 12th and 13th centuries. The Gudur inscription, and the Kaṭukūru inscription[21] of the Malyāla family are highly helpful in reconstructing the chronology of the Viriyālas. Even though 3 to 4 inscriptions of this family are found in the districts of Warangal, Khammam and Mahaboobnagar, they belong to the later period and no details are mentioned in them which are of help for our study. Clubbing together the information found in Gudur and Kaṭukūru inscriptions. Maliamāṁba, the wife of Malyāla Chaunda happens to be the grand-daughter of Viriyāla Malla, who himself was the great grandson of Kāmasānī and Eṟṟa. Thus it is possible to reconstruct the following genealogy for the Viriyālas.

Durjaya
|
Poṛaṇṭi Venna
|
Eṛṛa
|
Viriyāla Bhīma
|
Eṛṛa+Kāmasānī
|
Sūra
|
Prōla — Malla — Bēta + Bejjamāṁba
|
Sūra — Malla — Prōla — Komma
(under Malla)
|
Annaya + Aitamma
|
Mailamāṁba + Malyāla Chauṇḍa
(A.D. 1202)

In this genealogy we do not know the period of rule of each king. Even though, in the other face of the Gudur inscription, the Chāḷukya Vikrama year 49 was mentioned, it is doubtful whether that date also applied to the inscription of Malla in which the achievements of his ancestors are narrated. The definitely known fact is the date of Mailamāṁba and her husband Malyāla Chauṇḍa. In their inscriptions from Katukur and Koṇḍiparti,[22] in which their dates were given as Ś. 1124. Ś. 1125 and Ś. 1127, which corresponding to A.D. 1202, A.D. 1203 and A.D. 1205. As Mailamāṁba was only mentioned in the inscription of the year A.D. 1202, it is admissible to take that date as the lower limit for the chronology of the Viriyāla family. The date A.D. 1202, may be taken as the date of Mailamāṁba, and the preceding generations can be given 25 years of rule. Then the period of Kāmasānī and Viriyāla Eṛṛa ranges in between A.D. 1050-1075, and that of Viriyāla Malla in between A.D. 1125-1150. Thus in this reconstruction of chronology the individual dates of the members of this family are well established as follow :

1. Eṛṛa + Kāmasānī — A.D. 1050-1075.
2. Sūra — A.D. 1075-1100.
3. Bēta + Bejjamāṁba — A.D. 1100-1124.
4. Malla — A.D. 1124-1150.
5. Annaya + Aitamāṁba — A.D. 1150-1175.
6. Mailamāṁba + Malyāla Chauṇḍa — A.D. 1175-1202.

So we can possibly fix the period of Eṛṛa and Kāmasānī as A.D. 1050-1074 : of Sūra as A.D. 1075-1100 : and of one Malla as A.D. 1124-1150. These are the kings whose achievements are mentioned in the Gudur inscription.

To state in brief, the entire story, the conquest of Viriyāla Eṛṛa on the side of Boṭṭu Bēta, the protection of Kākati Bēta by Kāmasānī, and the help of Sūra in extending the empire all these belong to the period in between A.D. 1050-1100.

Now, in this light, let us turn to our main problem, the identification of Bētas mentioned in this Gudur inscription. As stated already, the Viriyāla couple and the Bētas must belong to the nearest periods, if not the self same period. The chronology of the Chāḷukyas of Mudigoṇḍa supplies us with only two Bētas who ruled from A.D. 1075-1100 and from A.D. 1125-1150. Among these two one has got the help of Viriyāla Eṛṛa in protecting his country, viz., Koravi. The chronology of the Viriyālas suggests, as shown above, that this event happened in between A.D. 1050 and 1100. Thus this date forces us to identify Bottu Bēta of Gudur inscription with Bēta of Mudigoṇḍa Chāḷukya family, who ruled from A.D. 1075-1100. As this Bēta happened to be in the list of rulers mentioned in the Kṛivvaka grant, there is no necessity to introduce another ruler of the same name as was opined by Dr. Parabrahmma Sastry.

Regarding the fourth and fifth stanzas of the inscription in which the help of Kāmasānī to Kākati Bēta, and the conquest of Sūra were mentioned, we can state that these events also happened before A.D. 1100 and after A.D. 1050. The then ruler of the Kākatīya family was Bēta II. To him only these services were made by Kāmasānī and her son Sūra. The help of Vaijadaṇḍādhinātha to Bēta mentioned in the Anumakoṇḍa inscription of A.D. 1117, is also in support of this evidence. Chronology permits us to connect these events with Bēta II.

Dr. Parabrahmma Sastry identifies Kākati Bēta with Garuḍa Bēta or Bēta I. The main difficulties in accepting Garuḍa Bēta as this Kākati Bēta are the following :

(*i*) Chronology does not permit us to do so :

(*ii*) Vaijadaṇḍādhinātha, the father of minister of Bēta II rendered the same help to Bēta II, which supports indirectly the championing of Viriyāla Kāmasānī on behalf of Bēta II :

(*iii*) Finally, the Gudur inscription itself does not mention Garuḍa Bēta. It merely mentions as Kākati Bēta, which term could be applicable to any Bēta of that family :

So we propose to identify this Kākạti Bēta as Bēta II on chronological grounds. In his younger days he was protected by Kāmasānī, and in his conquests he was helped by Sūra and Vaijadaṇḍādhinātha as this Gudur inscription and Anumakoṇḍa inscriptions suggest.

Thus to conclude finally, the two Bētas in this inscription are identified, the first with Bēta of Mudigoṇḍa Chāḷukyan family who ruled from A.D. 1075-1100, and the second with Bēta II of the Kākatīyas, who was his contemporary.

TEXT OF THE INSCRIPTION
(Telugu portion)

1. Anupama durjayānvaya su
2. dhābdi nanēkulu rāja nandanalu sani
3. na boraṇṭi Vennaḍanu saṁbha (Vu) ḍayye nati
4. prasiddhuḍai vinuta virōdhi māṇḍalika
5. vennaḍu vennuḍi vōle vānikini ghanu
6. ḍagu ne (ṟṟa) bhūpati jagadvinutuṇḍu (da) nuda

7. yihche gīrti tōnu// Bhāvita kīrtinaṭha (ta) niki
8. Pāṇḍava madhyama bhīmudō yanaṅgā (vi)
9. riyāla bhīma nṛipa ghasmaruḍai (yu)
10. di yinche vānikinu bhvinutuṇḍu
11. māṇḍalika bhūshanu deṛa narēndruḍu (tta)
12. ma śrī vinuntuṇḍu bandhujana sōvyvṇḍu
13. dānudayinche nunnatina // Ataṇḍani bo
14. ṭṭu bēta vasudhādhipu jēkoni vāni vai (ri)
15. nudhṛitamuna jaṁpi(ya) koravi dēśa
16. mu na(n) du pratishṭa jēsi tattaneyuru
17. pēru poḍagala dāyamu bi
18. ṭṭara gadyanaṁbu na pratimuḍu vāni
19. (chē) mogaḍupalliyu paṇḍraḍu nēlu
20. nappuḍē // Arudagunaṭṭi Eṛa nṛipu
21. (na) ṅgana gāmavasāni yoka mē
22. (lga) ruḍani bēta bhūvibhuni gāka
23. ti vallabhu chinnavāni dā baragaga jēta
24. baṭṭi ghanu ballavarāya niyō
25. gi jochchi bhāskaranibhu chakravarti
26. gani kākati nilpuṭa gōṭi sēyadē //
27. kāraka kāluḍai padase gāḍaya
28. nāyaku jaṁpi sūradavvēlupu
29. goṇḍa ravvanṛipu Vēlupu goṇḍa
30. na nilpi vānichē mēluga mūḍa
31. muppayini mēluga nēraḍu
32. bōṭipāḍu nuṁ mēlugu Tē
33. Kumāviḍlu mēluga reṇḍaya
34. rāju sangāḍlu]// sūtradhāri
35. Kommōjana barāha śrī śrī śrī
36. aḍapagaṭṭu dēvarakujanu

REFERENCES

1. *A. R. E.*, No. 108 of 1960-61.
2. *A. R. E.*, No. 107 of 1960-61.
3. *C. T. I.*, Part I, p. 15.
4. *A. S. P. P.*, Vol. 51 (1962-63), pp. 57-72.
5. *A. S. P. P.*, Vol. 51 (1962-63), pp. 73-84.
6. *Bhārati.*, 1975 May, p. 48.
7. *Andhra Patrika*, (Annual), 1970-71, pp. 6-32.
8. *Epigraphia Andhrica*, Vol. II, pp. 39-49.
9. *Bhārati*, 1972 May, pp. 45-49; *The Kakatiyas of Waaangal*, p. 147.
10. *Bhārati*, 1979, November, pp. 32-39.
11. *Epigraphia Andhrica*, Vol. II, pp. 39-49.
12. *Bhārati*, December 1979, pp-32-37.
13. *Inscriptions of Andhra Pradesh, Warangal Districct*, p. 145.
14. *S. I. I.*, Vol. X, No. 262.
15. *Inscriptions of Andhra Pradesh Warangal District*, p. 18.
16. *Epigraphia Andhrica*, Vol. I, 142.
17. *Epigraphia Indica*, Vol. V, p. 129.
18. *Epigraphia Andhrica*, Vol I, p. 121.
19. *A. R. E.*, No. 170 of 1966.
20. *A. P. A. E.*, 1967, No. 1.
21. *A. R. E.*, 1958-59, No. 86.
22. *A Catalogue of Inscriptions copied upto 1964*, No. 244.

5

FORGOTTEN CHĀLUKYAN FAMILY IN COASTAL ANDHRA

An important family that claimed its descent from the Chāḷukyas of the Lunar race is known from the inscriptions of Śrīkūrmam. Even though its members were not powerful enough to influence the contemporary political scene, they played a significant role as 'māṇḍalikas' in the local politics which was confined only to the present Srikakulam district.[1]

This Chāḷukya family of Śrīkūrmam connected itself with the Chāḷukyas of Vēṅgī and traced its descent from Vimalāditya who ruled from A.D. 1011 to 1018. Just because of the location of their inscriptions in the temple of Śrīkūrmam, we are mentioning this family by that name. But we are not certain that Śrīkūrmam was their capital. The political status of this family was also quite different from that of the other Chāḷukya families. They never established an independent rule of their own. They served as ministers and officers under the later Gaṅgas of Kaḷiṅga for more than four generations and played a notable role in the political

The order of succession and parentage in this list is further confirmed by the details about individuals mentioned in some other inscriptions. Hence there is no objection to accepting the above genealogy as reliable list of kings.

Vijayāditya I is the first known ruler in the direct line of this family. As stated already, his relations with Vimalāditya and Rājarājanarēndra are not known. V. Yasodadevi roughly calculated[12] the date of Vijayāditya as falling in the latter half of the 12th Century A.D., and allotted to his son Rājarāja a lengthy period of 73 years between A.D. 1200 and 1273. But from an inscription[13] dated A.D. 1273 issued by his son Vijayāditya, Rājarāja is known as a minister of Vīranarasiṁha of the later Gaṅga family who ruled from A.D. 1238 to A.D. 1263. Basing on this contemporaneity, we can fix A.D. 1250 as the probable date for his Rājarāja. Hence the date of his father Vijayāditya may be fixed in the period around A.D. 1225, a quarter of a Century earlier. Thus the periods of the first two kings viz., Vijayāditya and Rājarāja are fixed as A.D. 1225 to 1250 and 1250 to 1273 respectively. Vijayāditya II or Vijayārka, the son and immediate successor of Rājarāja is known from his record[14] dated A.D. 1273 from Śrīkūrmam. The latest limit of his reign is fixed as A.D, 1277 : as that is the date of another Śrīkūrmam inscription[15] issued by his younger brother Purushōttama. Purushōttama and his son Viśvanātha alias Jagannātha are the last known rulers in the pedigree. Purushōttama's earliest inscription[16] and latest inscription,[17] both located in Śrīkūrmam, are dated in A.D. 1277 and 1318 respectively. So the period of 41 years in between these two dates may be counted as the period of Purushōttama. But his son Viśvanātha alias Jagannātha issued three inscriptions[18] with dates A.D. 1307, 1308 and 1309 respectively. So it is not possible to fix him as the successor of his father Purushōttama, as Purushōttama's reign continued upto A.D. 1318. Hence Jagannātha should be considered as the conjoint ruler with his father from A.D. 1307 to A.D. 1318. But V. Yasodadevi thought[19] that Purushōttama stated in the Śrīkūrmam inscription of A.D. 1318 is probably the son of this Viśvanātha alias Jagannātha. There is little scope for this conjecture. We cannot definitely state that he was the son of Viśvanātha for it is not confirmed by any other strong evidence. After A.D. 1318 no rulers of this line are heard of. So the period of the five rulers of this line can be arranged in between A.D. 1225 and A.D. 1318, in the following manner :

Vijayāditya I	: A.D. 1225-1250
Rājarāja	: A.D. 1250-1273
Vijayāditya II or Vijayārka	: A.D. 1273-1277
Purushōttama	: A.D. 1277-1318
Viśvanātha or Jagannātha	: A.D. 1307-1318

Thus it is known that these princes settled in the area of Śrīkūrmam as ministers and officers in the court of the later Gaṅgas and continued to play an important role for four generations, roughly for a period of hundred years beginning from the second quarter of 13th Century. Though no details are available regarding the political history of this family, they must have administered the province under the Gaṅgas, though they did not date some of their records in the Gaṅga era or in the regnal years of the Gaṅgas.

Vijayāditya I is the first known ruler in this family. His son Rājarāja is stated to be a minister of Vīranarasiṁha I. By this time the Gaṅgas took an offensive step against the Muslims ; and probably they stood first among contemporary Hindu rulers to pursue an aggressive policy against the Muslims. It is Narasiṁha's conquest of the territory under the Muslims that provided him with the epithet 'Yavanāvanīvallabha'. It was probably that Chāḷukya Rājarāja also participated with his master in all these campaigns against the Muslims. His son Vijayāditya II is praised as 'the moon in the ocean of the Chāḷukya race' and compared to Indra in valour. But none of his achievements is known. Purushōttama, Vijayāditya II's brother, is described as a virtuous prince.

V. Yasodadevi attributes[20] to this Pursuhōṭtama an undated inscription in Drākshārāma[21] which mentions the gift by one Purushōttamamahārāja. But it is a mistake. That record itself states that it was given by Purushōttama of the Sūryavaṁśi Gajapati family. Moreover, it mentions the gift of land lying on the south side of Drākshārāma, a place where this Chāḷukya prince Purshōttama had no authority. The same writer, Yaśodadevi, notices another inscription[22] of A.D. 1287 in Siṁhāchalam and assigns it to this Purushōttama. The inscription however belongs to Purushōttamanāyaka of the Bhāradvāja *gōtra* and it is not correct to identify him with this Purushōttama, a Chāḷukya of Mānavasa *gōtra*. Moreover, the Siṁāchalam inscription states that Puruahōttamanāyaka was the grandson of Rāghavanāyaka ; whereas the grand father of Chāḷukya Purushōttama was Vijayāditya I. Thus, both the above said inscriptions of Drākshārāma and Siṁhāchalam are in no way concerned with this family of this Chāḷukyas.

It is stated that a set of peculiar copper-plates was discovered in the Purī district roughly six decades ago. These loose plates, which bear no ring were six in numbers. The first plate is inscribed on one side only. The contents of the first five plates are in verse. The inscription mentions the complete genealogy of the Eastern Gaṅga kings from moon to Bhānudēva II. The writing and the space left empty at the end of the fifth plate suggests that this genealogy of these rulers was kept inscribed on these plates for ready use in times of need. Though the sixth plate is of the same size and type which bears the same type of writing, it has no connection with the first five plates. It begins with a fresh invocation, dated in A.D. 1312, the fifth Victorious regnal year and mentions the name without titles of the king as Purushōttamadēva. It records the grant of several villages to 'Sandhivigrahika' Rangadāsa Śarmā who belonged to Vatsa *gōtra* and the kāṇva-*śākha* of the Yajurvēda. This grant was issued from his camp on the bank of the South Ocean, in the presence of Vīra Śrī Bhānudēva.

From this it is evident that this Purushōttama (of the Chāḷukya family) was in Pūri probably as a dignitary under Bhānudēva II. But

R.D. Banerjee identifies (*History of Orissa*, p. 278) this Purushōttama of the Pūrī plates as a different king, as the rule of Chāḷukya Purushōttama was over by that date and as his son Viśvanātha was ruling only the areas of Śrīkūrmam. He therefore proposes that this Purushōttama was a separate feudatory who usurped the throne of Bhānudēva II at about A.D. 1312. But it seems far from the truth. Purushōttama the donor of the the Pūrī plates need not be considered different from the Chāḷukya Pursushōttama referred to in the Śrīkūrmam inscriptions. While one Purushōttama as a subordinate of Vīra Bhānudēva is reported in the same period in the same area, it is necessary to think of another person of the same name who is not at all confirmed by any other evidence. As referred to already, his inscriptions are found in Śrīkūrmam with dates A.D. 1277 and A.D. 1318 respectively. By nominating his son to his seat in A.D. 1307 he might have gone to Pūrī to occupy a high position in the regime of Vīra Bhānudēva II. Banerjee suspected that this Purushōttama was a usurper who kept Bhānudēva II a prisoner. If it were so, why should he have stated in those Pūrī plates that they were issued in the presence of Vīra Bhānudvēa II ? Does it not indirectly show his subordination to, as well as his respect for Vīra Bhānudēva II ? Moreover the inscriptions of Śrīkūrmam dated around this period acknowledge the overlordship of Bhānudēva. Hence it is likely that Purushōttama of the Pūrī plates was no other than Purshōttama of this Chāḷukya family. But in this suggestion the main difficulty is its date. This Chāḷukya Purushōttama occupied the throne in A.D. 1277 as known from his Śrīkūrmam record. By the time of issue the Pūrī plates mention his fifth regnal year which indicates his date of coronation as A.D. 1307. But Viśvanātha or Jagannātha, the son of Purushōttama also issued inscriptions as a subordinate of Vīra Bhānudēva from A.D. 1307 from Śrīkūrmam. Since the same year has been mentioned as the date of cornation of his father in the Pūrī plates, it should be presumed that Purushōttama might have gone to Pūrī to occupy a better position in the Ganga court, leaving his throne to his son and successor Viśvanātha. Because it was a new position, he might have counted his regnal years only from A.D. 1307 in his record. If this presumption is correct, it can be said that Purushōttama resided in the Gaṅga court in Pūrī for more than ten years, i.e., from A.D. 1307 to 1318. In A.D. 1318 he came back to his original home, as known from his Śrīkūrman inscription bearing that date.

REFERENCES

1. *J. A. H. R. S.*, Vol. XXI, p. 62.
2. *History of Orissa*, pp. 259 and 289,
3. *E. I.*, Vol. V, p. 33.
4. *S. I. I.*, Vol. VI, No. 1000, 1002 etc.
5. *Ibid.*, No. 665.
6. *E. I.*, Vol. V, p. 33.
7. *Ibid.*
8. "Marugunapadda Vijayāditya Vaṁśamu-Tūrpu Chāḷukya Antargatamu", a paper presented to *A. P. H. C.*, Ramachandrapuram, 1676.
9. *S. I. I.*, Vol. IV, No. 1007.
10. *Bhārati*, Feb., 1981, p. 19.
11. *E. I.*, Vol. V, p. 31.
12. *J. A. H. R. S.*, Vol. XXI, p. 62.
13. *E. I.*, Vol. V, p. 33.
14. *Ibid.*
15. *Ibid.*, p. 34.
16. *Ibid.*
17. *Ibid.*, p. 37.
18. *S. I. I.*, Vol. V, No. 1214; VI, Nos. 1000, 1002.
19. *J. A. H. R. S.*, Vol. XXI, p. 62.
20. *Ibid.*
21. *S. I. I.* Vol. IV, No. 1362.
22. *Ibid.*, Vol. VI, No. 896.

6

BĒTA VIJĀYADITYA AND HIS SUCCESSORS

The Chāḷukya dynasty that ruled at Jananāthapura was one among the many ruling families that claimed descent from the moon and connected themselves with the Chāḷukyas of Vēṅgī. The rulers of this branch of the Chāḷukyas usually styled themselves as Sarvalōkāśraya Vishṇuvardhanas, the branded title of the Eastern Chāḷukyas ; and on many occasions the personal name of the king is ignored and the title only occurs. They ruled the area around Rajahmundry, Piṭhāpuram and Drākshārāma in the 12th and 13th Centuries. This branch claimed its descent from Bētavijayāditya or Vijayāditya V, the seventeenth rulers of the Eastern Chāḷukya dynasty of Vēṇgī. Their capital seems to be Jananāthapura.

The reconstruction of genealogy and chronology of the rulers of this family is not an easy task, as number of problems are involved in them. While dealing with this subject, the Government Epigraphist once declared that he was unable to reconcile

The death of Ammarāja Vishṇvardhana in A.D. 929 gave an opportunity for the subordinates and the relatives of the royal family to claim the throne for themselves with the help of neighbouring kings.[19] The right claimant, Ammarāja's elder son Bētavijayāditya or Kaṇṭhika Bēta, who had not yet passed the age of childhood, succeeded to the sovereignty of Vēṅgī. Some loyal subordinates and trusted commanders supported the claims of this boy king and opposed the disruptive and treacherous elements in the kingdom. Inspite of all these efforts Bētavijayāditya was not fortunate to reign long on the Vēṅgī throne. Tāḷarāja (the eldest son of Yuddhamalla I) and Vikramāditya (the younger brother of Kollābhigaṇḍa Vijayāditya) were the formost among the claimants. Their attempts to snatch the throne led to internecine warfare which endangered the country's peace and safety. It is said that they fought like 'rākshasas' and put the people to a lot of suffering.[20] Within a short period, Tāḷaraja defeated Kaṇṭhika Bēta in a battle. How he managed to overthrough Bēta and seize the kingdom, is not possible to ascertain. Probably he obtained the help of neighbouring powers like the Rāshṭrakūṭas. Inscriptions state that Kaṇṭhika Bēta ruled only for a fortnight and after this brief reign he was attacked, defeated and expelled from the country.[21] The Guṇḍugolanu plates of Amma II refer to Kaṇṭhika Bēta as having been captured by Tāḷarāja.[22] Thus the short period of rule of Bētavijayāditya of Eastern Chāḷukya family unfortunately ended abruptly. All this seems to have taken place in the winter of A.D. 929.

What happened to Bētavijayāditya after his captivity is not known. The records of this period do not suggest his death or his subordination to the victors. Some of them omit his name among the rulers. Some scholars have tried to identify this Bētavijayāditya with Bijja or Vijayāditya mentioned in the Vēmulavāḍa inscription[23] of Arikēsari II, and in the *Vikramārajunavijayam* of Paṁpa[24] and have suggested that he took shelter thereunder Arikēsari II. But opinion differs about this identity.[25] As opined by B.V. Krishna Rao,[26] no records of the Eastern Chāḷukyas refers to this prince as Bijja. In them his name is mentioned as Bētavijayāditya or Kaṇṭhika Vijayāditya only,

Moreover, Arikēsari rescued Bijja from the wrath of Gōvindarāja, the Rāshṭrakūṭa monarch. That Bijja or Vijayāditya belongs to the Mudigoṇḍa Chāḷukya family, and so he cannot be identified with this Bētavijayāditya.

Despite the unsettled condition of the kingdom and the insecurity for his life, Bēta Vijayāditya did not withdraw from the political scene. According to some scholars, Bēta wisely retired from Vēṅgī politics.[27] But this could not be true. He escaped from captivity and once again made his appearance in the period of the rule of his father's younger brother, Chāḷukya Bhīma II. In addition to Bēta, there were other claimants like Tāṭa Bikiya, Valaḍi, Munniṟiva, Rājamārtāṇḍa in opposition to Chāḷukya Bhīma II.[28] Chāḷukya Bhīma II gathered his strength and suppressed his rival kinsmen and their Rāshṭrakūṭa allies. Inscriptions mention that Chāḷukya Bhīma II killed many of them and drove Kaṇṭhika Vijayāditya again into exile in foreign countries.[29] Only the Māngallu grant of Dānārṇava asserts that Chāḷukya Bhīma II killed all these enemies;[30] but the Maliyaṁpūḍi grant of Amma II specifies that Kaṇṭhika Vijayāditya was driven into exile.[31]

Finally it appears that he returned to the country tried once more[32] to claim the Vēṅgī throne on the death of Chāḷukya Bhīma II, and opposed the accession of 12 year boy-king, Amma II. But it seems, this time also, as on previous occasions, his attempts met with failure.

The history of the dynasty upto two centuries from the time of Bēta Vijayāditya is a blank. Except for the claim of the later rulers that they descended from Bēṭa Vijayāditya, no related history of this dynasty is possible to construct upto Satyāśraya.

Nothing is known about this family from Bētavijayāditya down to the period of Satyāśraya. It is not clear whether in the intervening period members of the family, if any, ruled a part of the country with a subordinate status or shared the duties of administration in the royal court. Satyāśraya entitled 'Uttama Chāḷukya' of this line was the earliest known ruler. He issued no records and the date of his enthronement is not mentioned in any of the inscriptions of his successors. The only known fact about Satyāśraya is that his queen was Gaurī and that he had seven sons.[33] Gaurī was the princess of the Gaṅga family and might have been related to the Eastern Gaṅga king Anantavarman Chōḍagaṅga of Kaḷinga (accession in A.D. 1078) as was suggested by Hultzsch.[34] By her he had seven sons—Vijayāditya I, Vimalāditya, Vikramāditya, Vishṇuvardhana, Mallapa, Kāma and Rājamārtāṇḍa. Veturi Prabhakarasastry and Kasibhatta Brahmmayya Sastry[35] gave the list of these sons of Satyāśraya in a different way. According to them, the seven sons are—Trayīvīra, Vijayāditya, Vimalāditya, Vikramāditya, Vishṇuvardhana, Trailōkyamalla and Kāmarājamārtāṇḍa. In this list Trayīvīra was added and stated to be the first son and the name of Rājamārtāṇḍa was attached to Kāma, the sixth son of the list in the inscriptions. M. Somasekhara Sarma and M.V.N. Adityasarma[36] also deemed Vīra as the first son of Satyāśraya. But the word 'vīra' may be considered as an honorofic prefixed to the name of Vijayāditya. It should not be reckoned as the name of another son, but an adjective used to Vijayāditya as 'brave Vijayāditya'. The list of seven sons given in the inscriptions appears to be correct; and they are—Vijayāditya I, Vimalāditya, Vikramāditya, Vishṇuvardhana, Mallapa, Kāma and Rājamārtāṇḍa. Satyāśraya seems to have ruled from A.D. 1078 to A.D. 1118.

One important fact stated in the records of these rulers is that Kulōttuṇga Chōḷa I was not only the ruler over Vēṅgī but one who succeeded also to the Chōḷa throne. His immediate successor Vikrama Chōḷa who had the surname 'Tyāgasamudra' is said to have gone to govern the Chōḷa country. With his departure to Chōḷamaṇḍala, it is said the country of Vēṅgī became devoid of a ruler for some time. From this, it might be inferred that the Vēṇgī country was till then under the direct suzerainty of the Chāḷukya-Chōḷa emperors, Kulōttuṅga I and Vikrama Chōḷa; but then afterwards either the deputies appointed by the Chōḷa kings or those who appropriated that position for themselves ruled that country.[37]

Thus the inscriptions of this family belong to a slightly later period (roughly sixty years) and mention the departure of Vikrama Chōḷa to the South which occurred in A.D. 1118. They mention that, after his departure to the South, the country (Vēṅgī) became leaderless and chaotic ; and they narrate how in that period of struggle the Chāḷukyas of Jananāthapura snatched power. But contemporary inscriptions do not attest to this fact. Some scholars doubt[38] the genuineness of the statement of Piṭhāpuram pillar inscription and disagree with the statement that Vēṅgī becama rulerless after the departure of Vikrama Chōḷa to the South. They argue that it was a period of rise of the Velanāṭi chiefs; and, with their capital at Chandole, they ruled as subordinates and even as Viceroys of the Chāḷukya Chōḷas. Thus the claim of this Chāḷukya branch to have succeeded Vikrama Chōḷa in Vēṅgī had no basis. The inscriptions of this branch keep silent regarding to the rule of the Velanāṭi Chiefs in this area. They claimed their authority from Vikrama Chōḷa and did not mention the rule and authority of Velanāṭis who were the representatives of the Chāḷukya Chōḷas, The rivalry between the Chāḷukyas of Jananāthapura and the Velanāṭi chiefs of Chandole might also account for the silence of this inscription about the Velanāṭis. The information about their rise to power is noted not only in the Piṭhāpuram pillar inscription, but in their other grants like the Eḍarupalli grant and the Madras Museum plates.

Though the Velanāṭi chiefs established their power even before the departure of Vikrama Chōḷa to the South, they came into prominence only after A.D. 1118. A number of inscriptions suggest that the Velanāṭi Chiefs—became the Viceroys of Chāḷukya Chōḷas and ruled over the Āndhra. Their subordination is also nominal as some of their inscriptions do not at all mention the suzerainty of the Chāḷukya Chōḷas. The frequent attack of the then Chāḷukyas of Vēṅgī encouraged the ambitions and desires of the hitherto subordinate minor families ruling in the Gōdāvarī tract to declare their independence. This is attested to by a number of inscriptions of this period found in this area. This facilitated the rise of the Chāḷukya family of Jananāthapura. In that period of anarchy, in that period of keen rivalry for power, in that period of every-day warfare, the Chāḷukyas of Jananāthapura opened a new chapter in the history of Chāḷukyas as well as of the province by declaring their independence. They connected themselves with the Chāḷukya Chōḷas, who until then administered these areas. They recognised the suzerainty of Kulōttunga I upto the Viceroyalty of Vikrama-chōḷa. Thereafter, they began to give an account of their own dynastic history.

REFERENCES

1. *A.R.E.*, 1894, part B, No. 9.
2. *Historical Inscriptions of Southern India*, p. 382.
3. *E.I.*, Vol. IV, p. 226.
4. *I.A.* Vol. XX, p. 226.
5. *J.A.H.R.S.*, Vol. XX, p. 153.
6. *Ibid.* Vol. XXXII, p. 65.
7. *Bhārati*, January, 1968, p. 3.
8. *Ibid.*
9. *E.I.*, Vol. IV, p. 226.
10. *A.R.E.*, No. 10 of 1916-17.
11. *The Eastern Chāḷukyas of Vengi*, 164.
12. *I.A.*, Vol. XX, p. 267.
13. *J.A.H.R.S.*, Vol. XX, p. 153.
14. *Historical Inscriptions of Southern India*, p. 382.
15. *E.I.*, Vol. IV, p. 22o.
16. *Ibid.*
17. *Historical Inscriptions of Southern India*, p. 382.
18. *S.I.I.*, Vol. IV, No. 662.
19. *E.I.*, Vol. IX, p. 45, Vol. XVIII, p. 1.
20. *Ibid.*
21. *I.A.*. Vol. XX, p. 266.

22. *Ibid.*, Vol. XIII, p. 248.
23. *A.R.E.*, No. 170 of 1966.
24. *The Chāḷukyas of L(V)ēmulavāḍa*, p. 35.
25. *Pallavulu-Chāḷukyu lu*, p. 221.
26. *J.A.H.R.S.*, Vol. VI, p. 176.
27. *Ibid.*, Vol. XX, p. 153.
28. *S.I.I.*, Vol. I, No. 37.
29. *E.I.*, Vol. IX, p. 52.
30. *A.R.E.*, Cp., No. 1 of 1916-17.
31. *E.I.*, Vol. IX, p. 52.
32. *Ibid.*, Vol. XXIV, p. 268.
33. *Ibid.*, Vol. IV, p. 226.
34. *Ibid.*
35. *A.S.P.P.*, Vol. X, p. 42.
36. *J.A.H.R.S.*, Vol. XXXII, p. 65.
37. It is an interesting question whether Vikramachōḷa actually came to Vēṅgī as Viceroy. Except in the records of this branch of rulers, his viceroyalty is nowhere stated. A number of records in the Godavari district refer to Parāntaka as the Viceroy. Hence. B.V. Krishna Rao (*History of the Eastern Chalukyas of Vengi*, p. 466) identified both Parāntaka and Vikramachōḷa as one. He states that while he was is Vēṅgī he called himself Parāntakadēva, and when he ascended the Chōḷa throne, he assumed the name Vikrama Chōḷadēva. But there is no basis for this identification. Parāntaka might have been succeeded by Vikramachōḷa to the Vēṅgī Viceroyalty in A.D. 1118, in which year he was crowned as heir-apparent to the Chōḷa throne. From the evidence of the records of this family of the Chāḷukyas, there is scope to accept his presence as Viceroy in Vēṅgī for a short period in between A.D. 1118 and A.D. 1120, the year of his coronation on the Chōḷa throne.
38. *Bhārati*, September 1947, p. 267.

7

BRĀHMAṆAS IN MEDIEVAL ĀNDHRA

An important thing that Medieval Āndhra witnessed is the still continuing caste barriers and the predominance of the Brāhmaṇa community. In this article it is proposed to study the various details of this community. Brāhmaṇas occupied the highest position in society. According to tradition, Brāhmaṇas alone had the expert knowledge and competence required to perform sacrifices and rituals. They continued to be the custodians of the Vēdas, the Śāstras and other branches of learning. It was not merely their birth, but their scholarship that gave them the supreme position in society. There are frequent references to the high scholarship of Brāhmaṇas in the records and literature of the period. It is evident that they were the only highly educated people in society; and naturally people respected them. Adhyayana and Adhyāpana (Learning and Teaching) are the two-fold duties of the Brāhmaṇas. They were engaged in mastering the entire known literature on all subjects. They held all important offices in the State including those of ministers, revenue officials and military generals. They also officiated as priests in all domestic functions of a religious character and also in worship at the temples. Thus they held close connections with each group in the society. Though legal works like *Vijñanēśvarīyam* of Kētana[1] lay down some concessions and privileges to Brāhmaṇas, we do not know how far they were in actual vogue in this period.

Prior to this period and even in the period of the Chāḷukya of Vēmulavāḍa, other religions like Jainism made in attack on Brāhmaṇism, the religion in which the position of the Brāhmaṇas was supreme. With the outbreak of such non-Brahmanical schools of religious thought, the old traditional status of the Brāhmaṇas in society was adversely effected. It is known that a small number of Brāhmaṇa families, either because of the influence of the changing circumstances or out of genuine devotion to such new faiths accepted and joined them leaving aside Brāhmaṇism. Bhīma, the father of the poet Paṁpa, is stated[2] to have followed Jainism by leaving Brāhmaṇism. All the ancestors of his line were vedic scholars and Sōmayajins. He was the first to desert the fold. Conversion to a new faith, inits early stages probably did not bring any change in the caste. Jinavallabha, the brother of Paṃpa, though a Jaina, states[3] that he was a Kamme Brāhmaṇa. The term Brāhmaṇa indicates acceptance of the fourfold caste system; and it is a wonder how Jinavallabha, a Jaina, audaciously declared that he was a Brāhmaṇa. Nāgamayya, the father of Mallapa and Punnama, who encouraged poet Ponna is also described[4] as Jaina Brāhmaṇa. Thus we see that, in this period, Jainism could not prevent its members from describing themselves as of a particular caste. Gradually this tendency of clinging to caste disappeared with the emergence of new trends like Vīra Śaivism.

Regarding their approach to the Vēdic schools of thought, a majority of the Brāhmaṇas seem to have accepted and followed Yajurvēda. Though the followers of Ṛgvēda and Sāmavēda were also known their number was comparatively small. M. Somasekhara Sarma observes that the followers of Atharvaṇavēda were not found[5] in the records of the Reḍḍi period. The other periods in Āndhra make no exception. But in Eḍarupalli reissued grant,[6] one Brāhmaṇa, by name Dāmōdara, is stated to be a Chaturvēdin, a scholar, in four Vēdas Without scholarship in Ātharvaṇavēda, that term 'Chaturvēdin' could not have been used; and hence we may state that Atharvaṇavēda was also studied by Brāhmaṇas, but only by a very small number. A similar mention of the term 'Chaturvēdin' is also found in record (A.D. 1238)[7] from Dendulūru. In the copper-plate grants of this period a number of *gōtras* of the Brāhmaṇas were mentioned. Among them are the following:

Ātrēya	Kauṇḍinya	Śaunaka
Bhāradvāja	Kauśika	Śrīvatsa
Bhārgava	Lōhita	Śungabhāradvāja
Dēvarata	Maitrēya	Vadhūla
Gārgya	Maitravaruṇa	Vāśiṣṭha
Gautama	Mauna Bhārgava	Vishṇuvardhana
Harīta	Parāśara	Viśvāmitra
Kāmakāyana	Purukutsa	Yaska
Kaṇva	Rathītara	Maudgalya
Kapi	Śālankāyana	Kutsita
Kāśyapa	Śāṇḍilya	Śatha

In addition to these *gōtras*, there are also other sub-divisions based on *Rishi* and *Śākha.*

As this is a period of huge migration from place to place, another sub-division is noticed among Brāhmaṇas on the basis of their original habitation. Differences in political or religious approaches, natural calamities, or the favours showed by the rulers in the new areas might have been the causes for these migrations. It is said that poet Paṁpa, a native of Vēṅgī-*nāḍu*, went to settle at Vēmulavāḍa.[8] It is probably with a religious motive, as Jainism flourished better in Talaṅgāṇa than in Vēṅgī. In case these migrations were on large scale, the rulers provided accommodation to all those immigrants. A record of 9th Century at Ghaṇṭasāla mentions[9] the gift of dwellings made to 2,000 Bhrāhmaṇas. Bhujabala Siddhirāja alias Rāchamalladēva is stated[10] to have constructed 'Rāchamalla Chaturvēdi Mangalam' in the area of Nāgapaḍōlu in Pākanāḍu, to accommodate a number of migrating Brāhmaṇa families. Similarly, in the time of Vīrachōḍa, the son of Kulōttunga I and Viceroy in Vēṅgī, the migration of a number of Brāhmaṇas of the Drāviḍa country to the areas of Godāvarī delta is well a attested fact.[11] These mass migrations necessitated their forming into groups. This brought about another type of sub-division in the caste of the Brāhmaṇas, Which was based on their earlier habitation. This was no new feature in Āndhra. We find that these migrating groups with their crystallised sect-names joined the main steam of the Brāhmaṇa community by this time. A group of Brāhmaṇas hailing from a particular nāḍu or *vishaya* were named after that *nāḍu* or *vishayā*; for example—Velanāṭi Brāhmaṇas, Vēṅgīnāṭi Brāhmaṇas, Kammanāṭī Brāhmaṇas and Pākanāṭī Brāhmaṇas. Jinavallabha, the brother of Paṁpa describes himself in his Kurkyāla record[12] as a Kamma Brāhmaṇa, which means a Brāhmaṇa born in the Kammanāṭi Brāhmaṇa community. This kind of sub-division was in existence at least from the time of the Chāḷukyas of Vēṅgī, for an inscription of Ammarāja II records[13] the grant of an *agrahāra* to a Kamma Kulaja Brāhmaṇa, i.e., the Brāhmaṇa born in the Kammanāṭi Brāhmaṇa Community. M. Somasekhara Sarma opined[14] that the Brāhmaṇas of Kamma-*nāḍu* merged in the Brāhmaṇa community of Shaṭsahasrāvanī or Ārvēla-*nāḍu*, and of Karnāḍu or Karaṇi-*nāḍu*.

Regarding surnames, we do not come across any such mention in the case of the Brāhmaṇas in the early part of this period. This does not mean the Brāhmaṇas living in Āndhra at that time had no surnames at all, but they did not give any importance to them in the earliar period. Until the 13th Century the records in Āndhra, either lithic or copper plate, generally provide the names of the gōtras and the Vēda or Vēdas in which they were proficient and do not mention their surnames. In a record dated A.D. 1252 from Śrīkūrmam,[15] we find, for the first time, the names of a few Vaishṇava Brāhmaṇas along with their surnames, viz., Kari Kūrmanātha Śarma, Mudra Kūrmanātha Śarma, Jaṁpa Mañchana Śarma, etc. But there are a few early instances of the usage of surnames from the eleventh century, as could be seen in names like Pāvulūri Mallana and Koṭṭaruvu Kommana. Svāmi, Sōmayāji, Ārya, Śarma, Dīkshita, Shaḍanga. Bhaṭṭa, Dvivēdi, Trivēdi, Chaturvēdi, Paṇḍita, Ācharya, Ghaṭaśāsi, Bhaṭṭōpādhyāya, Yajva, etc. Where the terms used at the end of the names of the Brāhmaṇas as frequently found in the records and literature of this period.

It is already said that it was not their birth that brought these Brāhmaṇas a supreme position in the then society. They were generally learned in the Vēdic lore, Śāstras, Purāṇas and different branches of learning like Tarka, Nyāya, Mīmāṁsā, Vyākaraṇa, Jyōtisha and Gaṇita. The phrases, qualifying the donees, that find mention in the copper plate records bear testimony to the high standard of their learning and scholarship. Scholars like Viddana who is credited to have adorned all the assemblies of scholars in the town of 'Vāgīśaratnākara' was respected and honoured by a number of rulers.[16] Encountering no disturbance nor trouble from kings and their officers, these Brāhmaṇa scholars spent a peaceful life in their *agrahāras* by imparting knowledge to their pupils and spreading and maintaining the Vēdic culture and learning *Kāśīkhaṇḍam* and *Bhīmēśvarapurāṇam* describe[17] the prosperous conditions of Brāhmaṇas in the *agrahāras.* Some members of the Brāhmaṇa community constructed temples also. Viddanadīkshita is stated to have installed 'Śivajñānēśvara' at Bhīmavallabhapura.[18] The same scholar is stated to have regranted the lands given to him in the agrahāras of Puluparti and Uttarēśvara.[19] This type of re-grants by Brāhmaṇas is also referred to in the *Kāvyālaṅkāra-chūḍāmaṇi.*[20] Brahmadēyas, from which these Brāhmaṇas enjoyed revenue were generally exempted from all sorts of taxes. But this principle was not followed, in the 10th Century at least, in the case of bordering *agrahāras.* Sōmadēvasūrī in his *Nītivākyāmrita* lays down[21] that when the king had to make a capital levy in order to tide over a crisis, he could take a portion of the property of Brāhmaṇas, observing the only precaution that money absolutely necessary for the performance of the sacrifices was left with them. Brāhmaṇas who followed other professions like trade and industry were not exempted from any tax.[22] This itself shows that it was not birth but scholarship and profession that was respected.

To strengthen the validity of their claim on the granted *agrahāras*, the donees often declare that their's was *Śāsanada-agrahāras*. The possession of copper plate record governing the grant is its attestation. A reference to this is found in the Kurkyāla record of Jinavallabha. Pampa, his brother and the court poet of Arikēsari, states that his Dharmapura was the Śāsanada-*agrahāra*, but does not specify whether that was recorded on a copper plate or not. Jinavallabha not only specifies its character but also mentions the place where it could be found. Admonishing the importunate questioners, who wanted to know whether Arikēsari actually gifted the village to Pampa through a copper plate inscription and the latter accepted it, he directed them to go to Vṛishbhādri, where they could see the inscription registering the gift engraved on a lofty rock on the summit of the hill. This anticipatory reply of Jinavallabha itself points to the necessity and importance of recording the matter on copper plates while granting *agrahāras*.

It had become the self-imposed duty of the kings of this period, to recover and regrant to Brāhmaṇas, the old *agrahāras* which had been formerly in their enjoyment, having been granted to them by kings of Yore, but which were lost to them in the ravages of time. We have a number of evidences of the Brāhmaṇas who made claims about grants that were made to them by rulers whose names are preserved only in tradition and whose identity is not known. Repeatedly, in the various claims for the re-issue of the grants to the Brāhmaṇa donees, Mukkaṇṭi Kāḍveṭṭi alias Trilōchana Pallava is mentioned as the donor king of their respective original grants, that were lost.[23] A similar custom was followed in the Eḍarupalli re-issued grant[24] of Vishṇuvardhana of the Jananāthapura Chāḷukya family also. A number of Brāhmaṇas of various *gōtras* made a claim for the re-issue of the grant of Eḍarupalli, as the original document which was given in the time of Mukkaṇṭi Kāḍveṭṭi was damaged in the ravages of time. Presenting a claim for the re-issue of a document became necessary for them probably to inform the ruling authority that the family of the original Brāhmaṇa donee is still continuing to enjoy the land granted in perpetuity. There is reason to believe that, if these claimants did not do so, the government might annex their village also and draw regular revenue; or it could be granted for other similar purposes. One such event occurred in connection with the grant of Navakhaṇḍavāḍa, near Piṭhāpuram. It was originally granted[25] by Rājarājanarēndra of Rājamahēndravara to Pāvulūri Mallana, a scholar in Gaṇita *śāstra*, who lived in his court. For some generations, that village was under the enjoyment of that family. But after a period of roughly two centuries, Jayāmpika, a queen of Velanāṭi Pṛithvīśvara, gave it as a grant[26] to God Kuntī Mādhava of Piṭhāpuram. How a village previously granted to a Brāhmaṇa for a particular purpose was again offered to god Kuntī Mādhava by Jayāmbika, is an interesting point. It need not be considered as a mistake that took place in the royal archives. It must be the lack of legal claimants in the donee's family which led to the confiscation of that village; but a grant made by a king would not be taken back in any circumstances; and so the village must have been offered to the temple.

While some Brāhmaṇas endeavoured to preserve and propagate the Vēdic culture, some others came forward to bear the burden of the State. This difference in the nature of duties undertaken necessarily brought a division in the Brāhmaṇa caste, which manifested itself markedly during this period. As observed by M. Somasekhara Sarma[27] a 'laukika sect' of Brāhmaṇas came into existence. Though officers called 'Niyōgis' or 'Naiyōgika Vallabhas', were employed in the royal service from 7th Century onwards,[28] it is not known whether a separate sect emerged until 11th and 12th Centuries. This emergence led to the formation of two strong sects, Vaidikis (those who follow Vaidika Vṛitti) and Niyōgis (those who follow the laukika vṛitti) among the Brāhmaṇas. It does not mean that a Niyōgi Brāhmaṇa was precluded from acquiring the traditional learning. In fact, a number of Amātyas were referred to, as learned in the Vēdas and *Śāstras*. Veṅga Sachiva, the minister of the Chāḷukya family of Niḍadavōlu, is stated[29] to be a Chaturvēdin. Two inscriptions at

Bāpaṭla belonging to the twelfth century refer[30] to a family of the Brāhma-Kshatriyakula, i.e., the Brāhmaṇas who abandoned the traditional occupation of their caste and took to the martial arts of Kshatriyas. An inscription from Siṁhāchalam, dated A.D. 1393 also mentions[31] this sub-caste. It is observed during the middle Kākatīya period this section of Niyōgis gained greater influence in politics and higher social distinction; and in early post-Kākatīya period slowly crystallised into a separate sub-caste.[32] Yielding to the temptations of power and wealth they left aside family customs and traditions and got prepared to marry ladies of non-Brāhmaṇa ruling communities, as evidenced by the Indulūri-Kākatīya alliances. Thus they emerged into a powerful political section and held positions of importance like durgādhipatis, daṇḍanāyaks, etc.

There appears to have been a class of Brāhmaṇas who adopted trade as their profession, though their number should have been very small. An epigraph from Śrīkūrmam dated A.D. 1402[33] refers to one Rishidēśanāyaka of Kāśyapa *gōtra* as a brother of one Kaḷiṅga Vyāpāri. Though Kāśyapa *gōtra* is popular among the Vaiśyas also, this person is stated to belong to the family of *Upādhyāyas*; and hence to the Brāhmaṇa caste. A considerable number of Brāhmaṇas mostly of the Vaishṇava persuasion, were employed as temple servants in various capacities. An inscription dated A.D. 1102 at Vēlupūru (Guntur District) mentions[34] 'Dēvara Vaḍugulu', probably Archaka Brāhmaṇas who devoted themselves to the services in the temple. Joint families were rare as is sometimes supposed; for some of the copper plate grants which mention the specific share of the co-sharers of *agrahāra* villages, prove that in many cases fathers and sons were living separately.[35]

Thus, in general, a majority of the Brāhmaṇas, by their conduct and devotion to learning and *svadharma*, commanded the respect of the remaining Hindu society. But instances are not wanting of degeneracy, of loose character and morals of some of the Brāhmaṇas.[36]

REFERENCES

1. *Vijñānesvarīyam*, Verse 58.
2. *Inscriptions of Andhra Pradesh*, Karimnagar District, No. 3.
3. *Ibid.*
4. *Dakṣiṇa Bhārata Sāhityamulu*, p. 66.
5. *History of the Reddi Kingdoms*, p. 257.
6. *Bhārati*, Jan, 1986, p. 3.
7. *S. I. I.*, Vol. VIII, No. 737.
8. *Dakṣiṇa Bhārata Sāhityamulu*, p. 61.
9. *S. I. I.*, Vol. X, No. 19.
10. *Āndharula Charitra*, part II, p. 113.
11. *E. I.*, Vol. V, p. 70.
12. *Inscriptions of Andhra Pradesh*, Karimnagar District, No.3.
13. *Śārada*, Vol. II, p. 316.
14. *History of the Reddi Kingdoms*, p. 259.
15. *S. I. I.*, Vol. V, No. 1231.
16. *Bhārati*, June, 1979, p. 20.
17. *Kāśīkhaṇḍam*, Chapter I, Verse 37.
18. *Bhārati*, June, 1976, p. 20.
19. *Ibid.*, and *Epi. Andhrica*, Vol. IV, p. 110.
20. *Kāvyālankārachūḍāmaṇi*, Ullāsa, 5, Verse 29.
21. *Nītivākyāmrita*, Chapter XXI, Verse 14.
22. *Rāshtrakutas and Their Times*, p. 327.
23. *A. R. E.*, Cp. No. 4 of 1916-17; Nos. 779 and 803 of 1912.
24. *Bhārati*, Jan., 1968, p. 3.
25. *A. S. P. P.*, Vol. 52-53, p. 63.
26. *E. I.*, Vol. IV, p. 32.

27. *History of the Reddi Kingdoms*, p. 263.
28. *E. I.*, Vol. VIII, p. 239.
29. *S. I. I.*, Vol. VIII, No. 737.
30. *Ibid.*, Vol. VI, Nos. 127 and 156.
31. *Ibid.*, No. 1109.
32. *History of the Reddi Kingdoms*, p. 263.
33. *S. I. I.*, Vol. V, No. 1189.
34. *Ibid.*, Vol. X, No. 71.
35. *Rashtrakutas and Their Times*, p. 339.
36. *Krīḍābhirāmam*, Verses 244, 265, etc.

(*i*) Paleography suggests that this inscription belongs to the 13th and 14th centuries A.D.

(*ii*) Reference to Rājamahēndravara in this inscription suggests this to be a record of a later date ; and certainly not that of Vishṇuvardhana II ; who ruled in the 4th quater of the seventh century.

(*iii*) The other details mentioned in the inscription also force us to identify this to be belonging to a later date.

Vishṇuvardhana II ruled Vēṅgī in between A.D. 673 and A.D. 682. The *praśastis* given in his Āruṅthakūru[4] and Rēyūru[5] inscriptions completely differ from the *praśasti* portion of this Pedacherukūru inscription. More important than this is, that the Pedacherukūru inscription can be assigned only to the 13th and 14th centuries A.D. on paleographic grouds. Hence there is no possibility of identifying the Vishṇuvardhana of A.D. 13th and 14th Centuries with Vishṇuvardhana II of 7th century A.D.

The second important point is its reference to Rājamahēndravara. Rājamahēndravara was not known during the time of Vishṇuvardhana II. It did not exist then. According to some scholars, Rājamahēndravara was built by Amma I of the Vēṅgī Chāḷukya family.[6] *Kāvyālaṅkārachūḍāmaṇi* of Vinnakōṭa Peddaya of the 14th century said that it was founded by Chāḷukya Rājarājanarēndra who lived in the 11th century.[7] Thus by no means could the date of Rājamahēndravara be fixed prior to Amma I.

The next important point is about the epithets that were mentioned in this inscription. 'Vishṇuvardhana' and 'Praḷayāditya' were the important epithets that were applied to this king. No doubt, Vishṇuvardhana II bore these titles. But it should not be forgotten that there was a tradition by which the descendants of the ruling families adopted the epithets of their ancestors. This is borne out by a number of inscriptions. The epithets of his predecessors might have been similarly used by this Kumudavardhana.

The abovementioned scholars, Lakshmi Ranjanam and Venkatacharyulu, failed to explain satisfactorily the meaning of the word 'Kalyāṇabhūpati' of the time of Vishṇuvardhana II and related it with the Pallavas of Kāñchī which is untenable. Moreover, 'Kēsaripāṭi-gaḍa' which is familiar as a scale of measuring lands in medieval Āndhra was also mentioned in this inscription : and this goes contrary to their conclusion of dating the inscription in the 7th century. All these evidences go to show that the identification of Vishṇuvardhana Kumudavardhana with Vishṇuvardhana II of the Chāḷukyas of Vēṅgī is unwarranted.

The false date of the inscription itself is the main source from which arise all these problems. It is given in a Chronogram with the words *Gaṇēshṭanētra rasa dōh* to state the Kali year. It is not possible to calculate a figure from this chronogram. The details are not clear to help in this matter. If we take 'Ashṭa', 'Nētra', 'rasa', and 'dōh', as the words given, it shows the Kali year 2628. It corresponds to B.C. 474, a date which looks absurd in this context. With no explanation, the above writers Lakshmiranjanam and Venkatacharyulu attributed this date to A.D. 656.[8] Maremanda Rama Rao calculated this to Kali year 4982.[9] V. Yasodadevi mentioned this date from A.D. 1316.[10] But all these dates were mere estimations or conjectures ; and none of these writers explained how the conclusion is arrived at.

A copper plate grant which belongs to the self same Vishṇuvardhana refers to the gift of a village 'Ikshugrāma' to a Brāhmaṇa Nārāyaṇa Śarmā.[11] The characters of the letters in these plates belong to the 14th Century A.D. As in the epigraph, the date in the copper plate is mentioned in the same wrong chronogram of the Kali year, corresponding to Prabhava, with the details Māgha, Śu. 2, Thursday. The Government Epigraphist calculated the date from these details and fixed it as 14th day of January in A.D. 1328. This calculation can as well be applied to the Pedacherukūru inscription which bears the same Kali year and other details. Strangely enough the *Vaiśyapurāṇam* also mentions the same chronogram in connection with the grant of Tāmarāḍa.

Thus the Ikshugrāma copper plate grant, the Pedacherukūru pillar inscription and Tāmarāḍa grant mention the same Vishṇuvardhana.[12] He ruled the country with his capital at Rājamahēndravara, either independently or in subordination to any other power, in the period around A.D. 1328. Except these records, there is no other evidence in support of the rule of Vishṇuvardhana in the areas of Rājamahēndravara in the period around A.D. 1328.

TEXT OF THE INSCRIPTION

FIRST FACE

1. Svasti (//*) Śrīmatām sakalabhuvana saṁ-
2. stūyamāna māṇḍavya gōtrā-
3. nām hārītaputrāṇām kouśi-
4. kī vara prasādā labda rājyānā-
5. m matrugaṇa paripālitānā-
6. m svāmi mahāsēna pādānu-
7. dhyātruṇām bhagavannārāyaṇa-
8. prasāda samasādita vara varā-
9. ha lāñchana kshaṇa kshaṇa vaśī kṛu-
10. tārāti maṇḍalānām aśvamē-
11. dhāvabhṛuda stnāna pavitrīkṛuta vapushā-
12. m chaḷukyānām kulamalankarishṇa-
13. nija bhuja niśita nistriṅśa dhārāvana-
14. ta pratīpa nṛupachaya śi(ka)rōbhūsha-
15. ṇa mukuṭa taṭa ghaṭitha paṭu ma-
16. ṇi kiraṇāruṇita charaṇa yugaḷasya-
17. Śrī Vishṇuvardhana mahārājasya pri-
18. ya poutrahs navayuvati kucha kuṁ-
19. kuma paṅkāṅkita vaksha sthalascha narē-
20. ndra naravāhanascha tudirkkārāti (bhu)-
21. ja taru mūlōtpātana paṭu pra-
22. bhāva tva tribhuvana gaṅdha hasti-
23. puraṅdara iva gurvāmātyānuga-

24. tō vajrabhuchcha rāghava iva daśara-
25. tha nandajananō Vikramāditya i-
26. va rājanya vishama siddhischa yudhi-
27. shṭira iva Bhīmārjunādhika Kshamābhi-
28. scha bhṛihaspatiriva vachanīyya rāja-
29. vidyādharascha Tuṅga Taraṅga gaṅ-
30. gāṁbu nirmala yaśō mahita-
31. Yuvarājyasya Rāmadēvasya pri-
32. Yah/Anavārata lalitha mada mudi-
33. ta Vibhrama bhramita vanitā kaṭā kshē-
34. kshaṇa lakshitēshu/Makaradhvajō vṛu-
35. jina timira nikara vikaṭa vakratādi-
36. gdha ghanōdayēshu praḷayādi-
37. tyah prakaṭa prabhā(ta) di bhakshubhita kō-
38. lā hala sannaddha yuddhēshu vishama si-
39. ddhi dinanāthah suhrujjana dvijabandhu-
40. brundāraka mitra bhṛutya kānshita-
41. phala pradānēshu Kāmadhēnuh dēva-
42. dvija gurucharaṇa śi śrū (sha*) nābhiratah
43. Śrī Vishṇuvardhana mahārājah/a-
44. tha chāḷukya kulābdi sudhākarah
45. Kumudavardhana mānava nāmakah
46. jayati Rājamahēndravarēsthitō
47. ....śāsita...............
48. ....talaṁ.....................

SECOND FACE

49. ....hu-
50. Tava ha tri lō kān sa rugyaju(h) samamayō muditi-
51. Vēdastu śankhāni gadābjapāṇē// sakarodumbali hrudya-
52. sakra kavi hrutprahlāda rāhugraham bibrānam gaga-
nāta-

53. patramajadōh prakshāḷitō dvanghāṅgri ka(ṁ) Padmaṁ chakrama-
54. singadābja phalakāsvadvānghāngri dōrdaṇḍakaṁ dyāyē-
55. dasṭabhujam Trivikrama mahānādham Tribhaṅgīyutam// Sō-
56. yam mahāgnihōtrāṇām sapta satya samā-
57. nvitē/chārayūrou kruta vāsa ārābhya baliba-
58. ndhanāt/Pañchhāsat Kōti vistīrṇa mi-
59. la mārṇava mēkhalam/Daśāngu-
60. ḷa matikramya pādē naikēna tishtati/U-
61. rdhvanda maṇḍalabhōga chatra daṇḍa-
62. yītānghrayē/Brāhmaṇadatta pā-
63. dhyāya tīrdhapurah Kamaṇḍalōh/
64. bhūrbhuvasvatri lōkaika maṇṭapastaṁ-
65. bha mūrtayē/vakra . . . vaktra dōrda-
66. ṇḍavi patana patiyyesē/padama-
67. lingya bāhubhyam prahlādēna mahātmā-
68. na/Jayēna vijayēnapistuyamana-
69. ya Pa(ri)svatah/Kuśasuchi vinirbhinnabhru-
70. gu nandana chakshushē/vairōchanāvarōdha-
71. strivitīrṇābhayapāṇayē/Śrī Trivikra
72. ma nādhāya virādrūpa vilāsinē-
73. ghōra praharaṇōpētadīpta dīrghāsṭa-
74. bāhave/kamalākucha kāṭhinyagarva sa-
75. rvajya vakshasē/kalyāṇa mūrtayē Tasmē
76. kapaṭa brahmachāriṇē/Kastvam brāhmanna pū.
77. rvah kvacha tava vasati ryākhila brahma srushṭih
78. kastē trata hyanathah kva cha tava pita nai-
79. vātatam smarāmi/kiṁtēbhīshṭam dadāmitri-
80. pāda parimita bhūmi ralpaṅki meta trailō-
81. kyam bhāvagarbham balimidama vāda dva-
82. mano vassa pa yat/Svasti svāga-

83. ta matyaham kratupāteh kim diyya-
84. taṃ mēdinī/Ka matra mama vikrama traya-
85. mita dattaṁ jalam pādyataṁ/nō dēhētya-
86. sa...........rayam patram tatah (tō) shaṇam ta chchivam (bha)-
87. ......makha mukhē....................

THIRD FACE

88. sōpi digvijaya krīḍāḍaṁbarēṇa kshitī-
89. śvaram/sakalānapi nirjitya pratyāgantu-
90. (ṁ) samudyatah//Pūrvavaira manu smṛutya jitvā ka-
91. lyāṇa bhūpatīm/Tasyarājyā śriyam hṛutvā-
92. Yuddhē labda parākramah//Kiṁ chatrairupa sōbhatē mru-
93. ga patih kiṁbhairavasyāṁbarah Kiṁ nnandī na tṛuṇānku-
94. rārpita mukhah Kiṁ nō maruddhāvatī chāḷu-
95. kyānvaya Vishṇuvardhana bhavatpratyardhi pṛithvī bhujaṁhri-
96. mudra mapasāra yanti rahasi prouḍāvarōḍha-
97. striyaḥ// Tatramadhyē kshupuryāñcha stitva-
98. sāmanta vēshṭitah/Dādasan Śrīpatiṁārajavina-
99. Yōchita saṁbhramah/Kalyādyabjā gaṇēsṭa nētra-
100. rasa dō (ssa)ṅ khyē gatē vatsarē prāptēdha prabhavē ta-
101. pasya pi sitē pakshē ditvīya gu(rou)/ vārō
102. chēkshu purīndhranāma cherayūri grāma kē Śrī-
103. patiṁ natvānēna pura trivikrama rāmanādhā-
104. ya datta (ṁ) stitiṁ//Śrī Trivikrama balīndra śāsa-
105. na yarpitañcha cherayūrikēpurē (/*) khaṇḍa-
106. yuktamadha Vishṇuvardhana Khōnipēna Vihitam-
107. puratrayam/Unḍrālapālemithi pūrva-
108. talēcha khaṇḍam yaṁyañcha khaṇḍamidamō-
109. balasanipālem/Puṇḍrēkshanāma nagarē nara-

REFERENCES

1. *S. I. I.*, Vol. VI, No. 202.
2. *Bhārati*, Sept. 1972, p 12.
3. *Ibid.*, Oct., 1980, p. 14.
4. *I. A.*, Vol. VII, p. 191.
5. *Ibid.*, p. 185.
6. *History of the Eastern Chalukyas of Vengi*, p. 234.
7. *Kāvyālaṅkārachūḍāmaṇī*, Ullāsa 1, Verse, 4.
8. *Bhārati*, Sept, 1972, p.1 2.
9. *Inscriptions of Andhradesa*, Vol. II, Part I, p. 238.
10. *J. A. H. R. S.*, Vol. XXI, p. 27.
11. *A. R. E.*, Cp. No. 13 of 1961-62.
12. *Bhārati*, Feb. 1983, p. 42.

9

VISHṆUVARDHANA OF VAIŚYAPURĀṆAM

Literature and tradition, no doubt, play a notable role as the sources of history in throwing light on the dark problems whose course of events is not at all known through other evidences. But while accepting their genuineness, a thorough examination and verification with other sources is essential. In the history of Āndhradēśa, one problem that belongs to such category is the episode of Vishṇuvardhana Vāsavīkanya. One Chalukyan king Vishṇuvardhana who played a villanic role in connection with the capture of Vāsavīkanya of the Penugoṇḍa Vaiśya community is referred to in *Śrīvaiśyapurāṇam* otherwise known as *Kanyakāpurāṇam*. Hitherto the historicity of this Chalukyan king Vishṇuvardhana is considered to be entirely doubtful.[1] The writer of the *Vaiśyapurāṇam* in which the episode is described in detail is Guru Bhāskarāchārya, a resident of Penugoṇḍa, whose period is fixed by Śrī Kandukuri Viresalingam Pantulu[2] as sixteenth century. Basing on the dates given in the various versions of this work found in the

Oriental Manuscript Library, Madras, Sri Chaganti Seshayya[3] also assigned the date of Bhāskarāchārya to the sixteenth century. The reference to Bommera Pōtanāmātya in this work thoroughly confirms that it is a work of late date belonging to the period later than fifteenth century.

This traditional story, *Vaiśyapurāṇam* of the Penugoṇḍa merchant community is found in various versions. Its main version briefly narrates the story like this. At the instance of Śiva, merchants came down to the earth and lived in eighteen towns among which Penugoṇḍa stands as their capital. The other seventeen towns mentioned are Dharma, Dhanada, Pāñchala, Niravadya, Jananātha, Kshīrakāsāra, Dendulūru, Ēluru, Ghaṇṭasāla, Triguṇita, Ghana Bhīma, Viśāla, Kaḷiṅga, Nṛisiṁha, Vīranārāyaṇa, Āchaṇṭa, and Nagaram. One Kusumaśrēṣṭhi was the Kulapati of these Vaiśya families and he had a daughter named Vāsavī, who is stated to have been the incarnation of Dēvī Pārvatī. When she attained the age of seven the Chalukyan emperor Vishṇuvardhana, the father of Rājarājanarēndra, while on a tour through Penugoṇḍa chanced to see her, desired to marry her and requested the Vaiśyas to give their consent to the marriage. But as matrimonial alliance on maternal side is traditionally a must for the Vaiśya community of Penugoṇḍa, they were not in a position to accept the appeal made by the king. They feared that the king would victimize them, and at the instance of divine Vāsavī, all the elders of the Vaiśya community assembled at Penugoṇḍa and decided to sacrifice their lives by entering into firepits in order to protect their communal prestige and honour. Guru Bhāskarāchārya the religious priest of these Vaiśya families, encouraged them to oppose the king in protecting their traditional principles. He issued vīratāmbūlas in the assembly of Vaiśyas of all 714 *gōtras* and encouraged them to jump into the firepits instead of dying at the hands of Vishṇuvardhana. But in that assembly the Vaiśyas of only one hundred and two *gōtras* came forward to take Vīratāmbūlas and the remaining families decided to run away from that place. Vāsavīkanya cursed that the king Vishṇuvardhana would die as soon as he heard the news of her suicide, and she later on became a tutelary deity of the Vaiśya community.

At the request of the Vaiśyas of Penugoṇḍa at a later period, Bhāskarāchārya wrote the *entire* story as a Purāṇā in Telugu.

This is the course of events mentioned in *Vaiśyapurāṇa.* As said already the historicity of this episode is not above doubt. This is a late account written by Guru Bhāskarāchārya to enhance the prestige of the Vaiśya families of Penugoṇḍa under whose patronage he lived. Moreover this writer Bhāskarāchārya need not be identified with his namesake who is stated to have witnessed the entire tragedy. It is stated that, while preparing this work, he followed the original story previously narrated by Sālaṅkāyana. A number of scholars put it for severe criticism, as this work did not have any historical perception through it has much traditional value. They condemned the *entire* story as a myth created by Guru Bhāskarāchārya. Sri Chilukuri Virabhadra Rao[4] criticised this work, for, it was written with caste feeling and in a fanatic attitude. Sri G.R. Varma[5] observed that the figure of Vāsavīkanya in the temple of Penugoṇḍa seems to be a figurine of a young lady not one of a seven year girl as was told in the story. In the narration of the story also various versions confuse us in identifying Vishṇuvardhana.

Thus this is a story intended to enhance the prestige of the Vaiśya community of Penugoṇḍa. Those one hundred and two *gōtras* of the Vaiśyas are still considered as the *gōtras* of pure Vaiśyas ; and even now Vāsavīkanya is the tutelary deity of the Vaiśya community ; as such was its tradition we could not believe this work of sixteenth century to be the main origin of this episode. This is not basically created by Guru Bhāskarāchārya. He traced its origin from *Mārkaṇḍēyapurāṇam* in which the said king Rājarāja was stated to be of Śruṅgavaṁśa and to have ruled Māndhātapura. The same story is found in the *Navanāthacharitra* written by Gaurana. Either by mistake, or by an attempt to bring nativity to this story, the author Guru Bhāskarāchārya connected this to Vishṇuvardhana, the father of Rājarājanarēndra, the famous ruler of Āndhra who is already overloaded with the discredit given by the unfortunate episode of Sāraṅgadhara. The identification of this Vishṇuvardhana is the main difficulty in accepting the faithfulness and history of this *purāṇa.*

Though the historicity of this work and the identification of the said king Vishṇuvardhana is entirely doubtful, there is no scope to reject this story basically as mere legend. This episode may not considered as a part and parcel of history but one should not refuse its evidence as this is, to some extent, confirmed by other evidences. The internal and external evidence of this episode prove this as genuine by mentioning one Vishṇuvardhana in these areas at the time of this story. The reference to an important fact which related to the gift of the village Tāmarāḍa to Guru Bhāskarāchārya by the Vaiśyas enhances the historical value of this work. It enables us to trace the source and thus to search for the identity of the said king Vishṇuvardhana. It states that while Vāsavī and other Vaiśyas were entering into the sacred firepits in order to protect the traditional faith of their community, they issued a copper plate grant which registered their gift of village Tāmarāḍa, which was adjacent to Penugoṇḍa to Guru Bhāskarā-chārya. The text of that inscription is given in *Vaiśyapurāṇa* and it is dated in the chronogram "Kalyādyabja gaṇēshṭa nētra rasa druk saṅkhyē." The exact date is Thursday, Vidiya of the bright fortnight in the month of Māgha of the cyclic year Prabhava. As stated this was issued at the time of suicide of Vāsavī and Vaiśyas of one hundred and two *gōtras* and hence this date also stands to represent the period of the Chalukyan king Vishṇuvardhana, whose desire was responsible for the *entire* tragedy, in addition to this, two other records, Pedacherukūru pillar inscription[6] and the Ikshugrāma copper plate grant[7] which bear the above date give the details of Chāḷukya Vishṇuvardhana, the ruler of Rājamahēndravara. The Kali year, the cyclic year the month, the fortnight, the week day and the tithī of these two inscriptions are identical with the date mentioned in this Tāmarāḍa grant whose text is given in *Vaiśyapurāṇam.*

The Pedacherukūru inscription mentions that Vishṇuvardhana grandson of another Vishṇuvardhana is ruling these areas with capital at Rājamahēndravaram. It is stated that in connection of the earlier rivalry he made an attack on the rulers of Kalyāṇī and on their subordinate allies. While returning from that conquest he came to Cherukūru and granted three villages to God Trivikrama-svāmī. Previously scholars like Sri Khandavalli Lakshmiranjanam[8] and Sri Komanduri Venkatacharyulu tried to identify this Vishṇuvardhana as Vishṇuvardhana II of the Vēṅgī Chāḷukyan family who ruled in between A.D. 673 and 682. But this identification is unacceptable due to a number of objections. The paleography of thirteenth and fourteenth centuries found in the record, the reference Rājamahēndravara and the Chāḷukyas of Kalyāṇī, the reference to the use of Kēsaripāṭi-*gaḍas* in the measuring of lands—are the main difficulties in accepting his identification with Vishṇuvardhana II. Hence we have to identify this Vishṇuvardhana as a different king who ruled the areas around Rājamahēndravaram in the thirteenth and fourteenth centuries.[9]

The same Vishṇuvardhana issued a copper plate grant[10] which registered his gift of a village named Ikshugrāma to a Brahmin Nārāyaṇaśarman.

Thus the three records, Tāmarāḍa grant mentioned in the *Vaiśyapurāṇam*, Pedacherukūru pillar inscription, and the Ikshugrāma grant belong to the self-same period of one Vishṇuvardhana who ruled with his capital at Rājamahēndravaram. The Kali year, the cyclic year and the other astronomical details are mentioned in all these three in the same manner. But the peculiarity is that the three records supply us with a wrong date. The chronogram for the Kali year in them is "Kalyādyabja gaṇēshṭa nētra rasa druk saṅkhyā." The details are not sufficient to help us in this matter. If we accept Ashṭa, Nētra, rasa and drunk as the words given, then the Kali year became 2628. It corresponds to B.C. 474 which date is absurd for any Chāḷukya Vishṇuvardhana. Dr. Maremanda Rama Rao calculates this to Kali year 4928.[11] Sri Khandavalli Lakshminaranjanam and Komanduri Venkatacharyulu adjusted this to A.D. 656,[12] Dr. V. Yasodadevi mentioned this as A.D. 1316.[13] Thus scholars put forth various suggestions to supply a meaning to the above chronogram, but no one clearly stated how he came to that conclusion. But clarifying all these doubts, the Government Epigraphist calculated[14] the astronomical details in the Ikshugrāma grant and fixed the date as 14th January A.D. 1328. Since paleographically the two inscriptions should be dated in 13th-14th centuries, this is the only date in those two centuries which works out well for the astronomical dates[15] of the grants. This date could as well be applicable to Pedacherukūru inscription and to the Tāmarāḍa grant. Thus, it is now possible to say, in the light of the Pedacherukūru inscription and of Ikshugrāma grant, that this Vishṇuvardhana was a Chalukyan prince who ruled independently or dependently a small tract around Rājamahēndravaram in the first half of the 14th Century.

But against this conclusion, an inscription from Ghaṇṭasāla,[16] which is stated to have been one of the above eighteen towns, mentions the community of Vaiśyas of 102 *gōtras*. Since this record mentions the Vaiśyas of 102 *gōtras*, which number has its significance in *Vaiśyapurāṇa*, there is a possibility that this record was issued any time after the event of immolation of Vāsavīkanya.[17] But the date given in that record is A.D. 1164. Basing on this date Dr. K. Sundaram has stated[18] that the events recorded in the *Vaiśyapurāṇam* may be placed sometime before the twelfth century. But in the present discussion, basing on the evidence of other records, we have seen that A.D. 1328 is the date of Vishṇuvardhana. How the same number of *gōtras* of families who are related with the event of a later period could be described in the record one and a half centuries earlier is still a big doubt.

REFERENCES

1. *History of the Reddi Kingdoms*, p. 274.
2. *Āndhra Kavula Charitra*, p. 221.
3. *Āndhra Kavitarangiṇi*, p. 206, 9th Volume.
4. *Rājarājanarēndra Paṭṭābhishēka Sañchika*, p. 143.
5. *Bhārati*, May 1967, p. 29.
6. *A.R.E.*, No. 239 of 1897 : *S.I.I.*, Vol. VI, No. 202.
7. *A.R.E.*, Cp. No. 13 of 1961-62; No. 1 of Sewell, *A.R.E.*, Oct. 1890, p. 2.
8. *Bhārati*, September 1972, p. 13.

9. *Bhārati*, October 1980, p. 7.
10. *A.R.E.*, Cp. No. 13 of 1961-62; No. 1 of Sewell, *A.R.E.*, Oct. 1890, p. 2.
11. *Inscriptions of Andhradesa*, Vol. II, Part I, p. 238.
12. *Bhārati*, Sept. 1972, p. 13.
13. *J.A.H.R.S.*, Vol. XXI, p. 77.
14. *A.R.E.*, Cp. No. 13 of 1961-62.
15. Indian Ephimaries.
16. *A.R.E.*, No. 851 of 1917, para 84.
17. *History of the Reddi Kingdoms*, p. 274.
18. *Studies in Economic and Social Conditions of Medieval Andhra (A.D. 1000-1600)*, p. 61.

10

VAIŚYAS IN MEDIEVAL ĀNDHRA

One of the interesting things that Medieval Āndhra witnessed is the sudden upheaval within the caste and communal organizations of the lower strata. A great change in the attitude of the lower castes and their varied subcastes is remarkably traceable in regard to this period. The Vaiśya community of the then Āndhra, though not a neglected group, also made a bid to rise in the social scale. A brief examination of the circumstances that paved the way for their upheaval is the core of this paper. I have mainly restricted my study to coastal Āndhra during 11th and 16th centuries. I have utilized the information known from Telugu literature particularly from *Kanyakāpurāṇam*[1] written by Guru Bhāskarāchārya in the last part of the 15th Century, in addition to the details known by records.

The Vaiśyas of Āndhra are not a neglected community since ancient times. They were also known as Śrēshṭis,[2] Śeṭṭis[3] and Kōmaṭis.[4] How the term 'Kōmaṭi' originated, there is no satisfactory explanation. But *Kanyakāpurāṇam* states, because the Vaiśyas came down to the earth from the stomach of the Holy Cow, they are termed as Gōmaṭhulu.[5] One thing that is to be noted in this connection is this derivation may be fabrication of a later period for nowhere we came across the term Gōmaṭhulu for Kōmaṭlu in the records. Regarding their position in the society, though sources are scanty it can be said that they were in a prosperous condition. They chose the profession of trade and commerce which made them rich and also connected them with each group of society. For purposes of either purchase or sale, they travelled throughout the land and held their organizations everywhere.[6] They established guilds and such other caste oriented or profession oriented bodies and strengthened themselves with its background. Thus economically and professionally they were sound. Some sources like the Ahadanakaram record[7] which belongs to the period of the Chāḷukyas of Vēṅgī, though traced the guild activity, the details regarding their status in the society is not known. As such was their earlier position, in the earlier parts of the medieval period a sudden phenomenon happened in the social system at lower levels and this affected basically the entire society, in particular the community of the Vaiśyas.

Until 10th Century the Śūdras who lived in the lower strata of the society did not aspire high status. They seem to have been content with their position. As artisans, as cultivators, they chose many a profession and stood as the backbone of the economy of the period. But with the political unrest and in the internecine warfare that took place after the downfall of the Chāḷukyas of Vēṅgī, these Śūdra families entered into politics. Even earlier to this period some of the members of the fourth caste distinguished themselves by their bravery and skill in the art of warefare, became reputed generals and officers of state. By this time they esta- the blished kingdoms and exercised their authority. To this category belong families like the Velanāṭis, Kōṭas, Koṇḍapaḍumaṭis, Kākatīyas, Rēcherlas, Koppula Chiefs, Reḍḍis and some petty chieftains in the lower Gōdāvarī valley. With such an establishment of power in some regions of Āndhra the Śūdras emerged as rulers; and this new status enabled them to come nearer to the upper castes. In the guise of power they contracted alliances of marriage with the Kshatriyas and even with the Brāhmaṇas. Sri M. Somasekhara Sarma noticed[8] a great change in the attitude of the civil law, with the rise of the Śūdras of this period to political power. Previously the right to make a gift of land either to the temple or to a Brāhmaṇa rested only in the ruling authority according to the Dharma-*śāstras*. But some of these rulers were either overlooked or disregarded, when these Śūdra communities rose to power. In the period of Śūdra political ascendancy any one and every one, who desired to make such a gift, did so even without the formal sanction of the king. Similarly until then, Śūdra communities were not allowed to study Sanskrit literature. This period witnessed the Śūdra's study and sometimes composition of the Sanskrit works. This was indeed a great change. This attests to the internal desire and zeal for rights and privileges of the Śūdras who were suppressed in some respects until then. They imitated the Chiefs and Potentates and assumed different titles likewise. Almost every important community like the Balāñjas,[9] Viśvakarmas[10] and Telikis[11] had this kind of *Praśastis* recorded in their inscriptions. It would seem that almost all these professional classes in the Śūdras associated themselves with a place which they considered as their original home, and boasted of themselves as lords of one particular town. Each of these communities busied itself with inventing a mythical origin for itself. They went to the extent of deriving their origin from the Celestial Beings. This was perhaps with a view to outdo the Brāhmaṇas. The Brāhmaṇas traced their origin from sages, who are mortals. In claiming their origin to Celestial Beings, these communities expected superior treatment and held claims to the privileges that were enjoyed by the upper classes like the Brāhmaṇas. On the basis of soundness of these claims, this may be considered as a movement within the caste system by the lower castes to upgrade themselves. This movement, inspite of its drawbacks, made the common people to realise their power and infused self-confidence in them. In the light of this change in the attitude of the Śūdras, let us study the response of the Vaiśyas in regard to the betterment of their position in the society.

The Vaiśyas are given the third place in the traditional social set-up, whereas the Śūdras occupied the fourth place. In the fourfold caste organization, the duty of the Vaiśyas was trade and commerce and the duty of the Śūdras was cultivation and handicrafts. But as stated above, the Śūdras who were not satisfied with their social status tried to upgrade their social position. By this time, the conditions of the upper castes also favoured their decision. With the downfall of the Chāḷukyan authority in Telugu-*nāḍu*, or even in their period the Vēdic rituals were relegated to a secondary place and the Brāhmaṇas took up various professions in addition to imparting knowledge to the pupils. The position of the Kshatriyas was also not encouraging. The country of Āndhras became 'anāyakam' as Vikramachōḍa, the son of Kulōttunga I went to the South to rule the Tamil country.[12] Though some Kshatriya families tried to restore their authority. they succeeded in occupying only small portions of the country.[13] Taking this as an advantage, Śūdras who were waiting for an opportunity established kingdoms and began to rule the country. With this Śūdra ascendancy to power, all the three castes except that of Vaiśyas enjoyed the taste of power. This new change might have probably pinched the hearts of the Vaiśya community. The Śūdras who were next to them in the social order superseded them, discharged the powers of the Kshatriyas and established themselves as the ruling authority. Inspite of their wealth, inspite of their vast organizations, inspite of their command over the imports and exports, they remained where they were in the social position. Until then they were contented with the acquisition of more and more property and wealth. But the advancement of the Śūdras encouraged and drove them towards power and new claims for social status. As soon as they realised that power was more essential than money, they started their attempts to enter into the field of administration.

As stated already, trade was the main profession of this community. It brought them more riches and hence naturally they were given importance on some occasions. They were respected in the royal courts. An epigraph of 10th Century from Vēmulavāḍa in the Karimnagar district refers[14] to a band of nine Śrēshṭis along with other important elders of the royal court. This is the earliest epigraphical evidence that mentions a dignitary position of the Vaiśyas in Āndhra. With such backing of their property and position in the society, this community of Vaiśyas entered into royal service and joined as bankers and treasurers to the royal courts. A record of the 12th Century describes[15] one Penugoṇḍa merchant as having served the needs of the Velanāṭi Chōḍa king Goṅka II. Śrīnātha's *Haravilāsam* which was dedicated to Avachi Tippayya Śeṭṭi, states[16] that Tippayya Śeṭṭi's family was in the service of the Reḍḍi rulers of Koṇḍavīḍu, Dēvaya Śeṭṭi, father of Tippaya Śeṭṭi is said to have acted as a Śeṭṭi to Vēmārḍḍi. He was the banker of Vēmāreḍḍi and financed him for building steps to Śrīśailam and Pātāḷagaṅga, and probably for raising armies. Tirumala Śeṭṭi the brother of Tippaya Śeṭṭi used to serve king Kumāragiri and was equally in touch with other important rulers of the time, Harihararāya of Vijayanagar, Ferj Shah of Bahmani kingdom and the Gajapati of Orissa. Tippaya Śeṭṭi was the greatest of all and he even received *insignia* of royalty and different titles from king Kumāragiri. Thus there are number of instances of their entering into the royal courts. As they were already the masters in the art of money dealings, they used to win over the rulers to their side. This made them to extend their fields of service into administration. Some of them were appointed as Mahāsēnāpatis and Mahāpātras. A record of 14th Century from Sīṁhāchalam mentions[17] one Gurudāsa of Vaiśya kula as a Mahāsēnāpati. In another record one Śrīkaraṇa Mahānādha Sēnāpati of the Vaiśya community is mentioned[18] as Śēnādhyakshavara and as the governor of the Southern Kaḷiṅga province under the later Gaṅgas. They seem to have been conferred the royal *insignia* of office like horse, umbrella, Alavanṭuka, Kañche, Kīlavaṭṭa, etc.[19] They bore distinctive epithets. Jagadobbagaṇḍa, Paḍirāya, Dēśiśeṭṭi, etc. are the titles that frequently figure in records.[20] Occasionally they were granted *agrahāras* also.[21] Thus within a short period they succeeded in acquiring a status of their own in the administrative set-up.

Regarding the so-called social status, they have already acquired it through their riches and guild activities. But they had no traditional glory and ancestry which are claimed even by the lower groups in the society like the Telikas, Balañjas and the Viśvakarmas. Though they had the initiation ceremony as per the Vēdic injunction and could have had the *gōtras* of the *ṛishis*, the early Āndhra records are conspicuous of their absence. But during this period, with a view to enhance their glory they claimed many more *gōtras* from various sages. The *Haravilāsam*, which was dedicated to Avachi Tippayya Śeṭṭi by Śrīnātha, refers to thousand *gōtras* of the Vaiśyas.[22] In the *Kanyakāpurāṇam* by Guru Bhāskarāchārya, it is said that the Vaiśyas belong to 714 *gōtras* among which 200 *gōtras* consist of Bhārgavaṛishi gaṇa, 252 consist of Śāṇḍilyaṛishi gaṇa, 66 consist of Prabhātaṛishi gaṇa and the remaining 196 consist of Kāśyapaṛishi gaṇa. An elaborate list of a number of these *gōtras* is given in that *purāṇa* and they tally with names of the *gōtras* of the Vaiśyas found in the inscriptions.

The *Kanyakāpurāṇam* gives us an account of communal history of the Vaiśyas not known from other sources. The Vaiśyas were the devotees of god Nagarēśvaradēva. In all Vaiśya towns there is a temple of Nagarēśvara. According to the *purāṇa*, Lord Śiva while instructing the Vaiśyas to leave the Heaven to take up residence on the earth so that the earth might be lifted from the morass of poverty in which it was sunk on account of their absence, promised, as compensation for their loss of heavenly residence, that he would assume the form of Nagarēśvara to be particularly worshipped by the Vaiśyas. According to the *Purāṇa*, there are 18 towns that constituted the original habitat of the all Vaiśyas of 714 *gōtras*. The names of those towns and the respective names of the families which resided in them are given in it. In that list towns like Viśākha, Āchanṭa, Dhanada, Ghaṇṭasāla, Pīṭhikāpura and Penugoṇḍa could be identifiable with the present Visakhapatnam, Achanta, Chandavolu, Ghaṇṭasāla, Piṭhapuram and Penugoṇḍa, the towns in the coastal Āndhra. But the places like Dharma, Pāñchāla, Triguṇa, Vīranārāyaṇa and other are not yet identified. The Vaiśyas of Āndhra seem to have formed themselves into a corporate community with their principal seat at Penugoṇḍa in west Godavari district. Since all these places are situated in proximity and since there are instances of merchant of one place visiting another place, it is reasonable to suppose that the communal organization visualised in the *Kanyakāpurāṇa* might save survived to bind these Vaiśyas into a compact body. Probably the 'nakaram' at Penugoṇḍa looked to the general interests of the *entire* community of the Vaiśyas. In the case of critical issues, they could be settled at a meeting of the assembly comprising all the heads of the Nagaras.

Interestingly, the *Purāṇa* narrates a crucial event that happened at Penugoṇḍa which put the whole community to a severe test out of which only Vaiśyas of 102 *gōtras* emerged successfully. One king Vishṇuvardhana of the Rājamahēndravaram while on tour, came to Penugoṇḍa, chanced to see Vāsavīkanya, the daughter of Kusuma Śeṭṭi, the chief Śeṭṭi residing at Penugoṇḍa. He fell in love with her and asked the Vaiśyas to give her in marriage to him. But this request was utterly rejected.[23] In the assembly of the Vaiśyas, some expressed the opinion that to agree to marry the girl to a Kshatriya would be a sacrilage and against the caste rule of 'mēnarikam' of the Vaiśya community.[24] But it appeared that they could not live as the king became insistent in having the girl married to him. So on the advice of their priest Bhāskarāchārya, they decided to sacrifice there lives for honour. This, however, did not meet the approval of all and among the total number of 714 *gōtras*, the families of 612 *gōtras* decided to leave their kinsmen and to live separately in the other parts of the country. Thenceforward the Vaiśyas of the remaining 102 *gōtras* whose elders entered into firepits along with Vāsavī, came to be regarded as the pure *gōtras* of the Vaiśyas. Even now in the Āndhra country, those 102 *gōtras* of Vaiśyas are considered to be the pure Vaiśyas, and even now their tutelary deity is Vāsavīkanya of Penugoṇḍa in the West Godavari District. Offenders against the social conventions of the Vaiśyas caste who as a consequence, had been excommunicated could be brought back into the fold of the community through an elaborate and costly *prāpaśchitta* ceremony which is stated at length in the *purāṇa*. Though this work belongs to 15th Century, there is independent evidence of the epigraphs[25] beginning from 12th Century regarding donations in various places of merchants with different *gōtras*, who describe themselves as the lords of Penugoṇḍa, celebrating the importance of Penugoṇḍa, which is depicted in the *Purāṇa*. Moreover an inscription of 16th Century from Uṇḍavalli gives an interesting information about the Lords of Penugoṇḍa that has some connection with the above *purāṇa*.[26] It states that they erected a temple to God Bhāskarīśvara at Uṇḍavalli, and made arrangements for the daily services of the God. It is plausible that these Vaiśyas installed that deity in the name of the guru of their community which is known from the *purāṇa*.

Though the historicity of the *Kanyakāpurāṇa* is not unquestionable,[27] it is most important and unique source of information regarding the social life of the Vaiśyas in Āndhra. Art of business, following Dharma, protecting cows, obtaining expertise in examining all the commodities even diamonds, are stated to be chief characteristics of the Vaiśyas.[28] A record of 12th Century describes the Penugoṇḍa merchants in glowing terms.[29] They were the followers of Dharma and obtainers of the grace of the wise. They were endowed with kindliness and they pleased all people by their acts. They belonged to the race of Kubēra, with fame spread all over the world. Their skill in examining gems and diamonds is also attested in an epigraph of 15th Century in Āndhra.[30] Being enriched with the wealth obtained through various sorts of business some of the Vaiśyas, according to the *Purāṇa*, claimed superiority over the Kshatriyas. They put forward a question that in what aspect the kings were superior to them.[31] They reminded that their community was everywhere in the country and held command over all trade and commerce. They said that they need not obey the orders of the kings. They prefer to follow Kula-*dharma* even at the cost of any. In protecting that, they even come to sacrifice their lives. Though they respected Brāhmaṇas and offered them grants, it seems that they were denied vedic rituals. They wished to prohibit the vedic rituals like Aśvamēdha, Gōmēdha, Jyeṣṭabhāga, Palalaśrāddha, etc., along with the social reforms like widow remarriage and intercaste marriage.[32] They no more desire to follow vedic mantras. Instead of vēdavidhi, they wished to follow puraṇōktavidhi. Even then, their non-vedic ideology by no means turned them against the Brāhmaṇas. Moreover, some of the stated themselves as 'Śrōtriyas'. A record of the 12th Century from a place near Ādoni refers to one Eṛeya-maśeṭṭi as a great merchant of the Śrōtriya family.[33] *Vaiśya Vaṁśasudhākaram* also states[34] that Vaiśyas are entitled to the privileges of Svādhyana, Yajana, Dāna of marrying within their own caste, and of following the occupations of trade, agriculture and tending cattle. The Vaiśyas offered grants to Brāhmaṇas and, even in *Kanyakāpurāṇam* itself, it is stated the various rates of amounts the Vaiśyas have to offer to their purōhitas.[35] It states that all the Vaiśyas have to honour the purōhitas by offering 8 *varahās* on his annual visit, 12 *varahās* in the time of marriages, 6 *varahās* on the occasion of Sīmanta, 3 *varahās* on the occasion of Garbhādāna, 6 *varahās* on the occasion of Puṁsavana respectively. On the occasion of the birth of a boy 3 *māḍas* are to be given and if the child is a girl the amount to purōhita is only 1½ *maḍās*. Moreover in the time of partition of property among brothers and in the transaction of purchase and sale, dharmāṁśa, a small portion in the profit is also offered. Similar such practices are common even now in the community of Vaiśyas.

In the above study, it can be observed that the *Kanyakāpurāṇam* of 15th Century, is a useful work throwing light on the conventions of the Vaiśyas and their status in society, which is otherwise unknown. Though epigraphs refer to their role in the fields of economy and religion, their social life in Āndhra is not forthcoming from it. It is interesting that the practices of 15th Century or even earlier, are still in vogue among the Vaiśyas of Āndhra. The conditions which favoured the emergence of the Śūdras to power in Āndhra could not be otherwise for the Vaiśyas as well to advance their equal, if not superior, claims in society. Owing to the wealth they possessed, they could remain as an exclusive community without much interaction with other communities in matters of marriage, etc. while Brāhmaṇas and Kshatriyas were intermingling with Śūdras.

REFERENCES

1. *Śrī Vāsava Kanyakāpurāṇam*, published by Ārya Vaiśya Yuvajana Sanghamu (Penugonda, 1951).
2. *A.R.E.*, No. 170 of 1966.
3. *A.R.E.*, No. 455 of 1899.
4. *S.I.I.*, Vol. VI, No. 87.
5. *Kanyakāpurāṇam*, Chapter 54, stanza 45.
6. R. Narasimha Rao, *Corporate Life in Medieval Andhra*, p. 33.
7. *Studies in Indian Epigraphy*, Vol. I, p. 124.
8. M. Somasekhara, *History of the Reddi Kingdoms*, p. 277.
9. K. Sundaram, *Studies in Economic and Social Conditions of Medieval Andhra* (*A.D. 1000-1600*), p. 70.
10. *S.I.I.*, Vol. VI, No. 209.
11. *E.I.*, Vol. VI, p. 334.
12. *Ibid.*, Vol. VI, p. 226.
13. *Ibid.*
14. *A.R.E.*, No. 170 of 1966.
15. *S.I.I.*, Vol. IV, No. 1131.
16. M. Somasekhara Sarma, *History of the Reddi Kingdoms*, p. 272.
17. *S.I.I.*, Vol. VI, No. 853.
18. *Ibid.*, Vol. V, No. 1284.
19. *Ibid.*, Vol. IX, No. 41.
20. *Ibid.*, Vol. VI, No. 955.
21. *A.R.E.*, No. 165 of 1959-60.
22. *Haravilāsam*, Chapter II, stanza 139.

23. *Kanyakāpurāṇam*, Chapter 32, stanzas 12, 13.
24. *Ibid.*, Chapter 40, stanzas 53, 54.
25. *A.R.E.*, Nos. 701, 702, 703 of 1926; *S.I.I.*, Vol. X, Nos. 114, 115, 264, etc.
26. *S.I.I.*, Vol. X, No. 737.
27. The historicity of *Kanyakāpurāṇam* is discussed in my paper "Vishṇuvardhana and Vāsavīkanya" presented at the Andhra Pradesh History Congress, VI Session held at Hyderabad, 1982.
28. *Kanyakāpurāṇam*, Chapter 24, stanza 9.
29. *S.I.I.*, Vol. X, No. 82.
30. *A.R.E.*, 1918, para 85.
31. *Kanyakāpurāṇam* Chapter 35, stanzas 47-48.
32. *Ibid.*, Chapter 36, stanzas 29-30.
33. *A.R.E.*, No. 504 of 1915.
34. *New Indian Antiquary*, Vol. II, p. 442.
35. *Kanyakāpurāṇam*, Chapter 44, stanzas 25-27.

BIBLIOGRAPHY

I. PRIMARY SOURCES

(i) *Epigraphy*

Annual Reports of South Indian Epigraphy, 1887-1945.

Annual Reports on Indian Epigraphy.

Andhra Pradesh Annual Report on Epigraphy, 1965, 1966 and 1967.

A Topographical List of Inscriptions in the Madras Presidency 3 volumes, by V. Rangacharya, Madras, 1919.

Copper Plate Inscriptions in the Hyderabad Museum, Vol. I, Edited by N. Ramesan, Hyderabad, 1962.

Corpus of Telingana Inscriptions, parts I, II and III, edited by Dr. P. Srinivasachar, Hyderabad, 1940, 1958 ; Vol. IV, by M. Somasekhara Sarma, Hyderabad, 1973.

Epigraphia Āndhrica.

Epigraphia Indica.

Inscriptions of Andhra Pradesh : Karimnagar, Warangal Districts.

Inscriptions of Andhradesa, Edited by Dr. M. Rama Rao.

Journal of the Epigraphical Society of India.

Kannada Inscriptions of Andhra Pradesh, edited by Dr. P. Srinivasachar and Dr. P.B. Desai, Hyderabad, 1961.

Stone and Copper Plate Inscriptions of the Nellore District, 3 volumes by Butterworth and Venugopala Chetty, Madras, 1905.

South Indian Inscriptions, Volumes, IV, V, VI, VII and X.

Select Epigraphs of Andhra Pradesh, edited by P.V. Parabrahma Sastry, Hyderabad, 1965.

Select Stone Inscriptions of Andhra Pradesh Government Museum, edited by P.B. Desai, Hyderabad, 1962.

The Historical Inscriptions of Southern India and Outlines of Political History, by R. Sewell, edited by S. Krishna Swami Aiyangar, Madras, 1932.

(ii) *Literature*

Bhāskarāchrya : *Śrī Vāsava Kanyakāpurāṇamu* Penugoṇḍa, 1951.

Mañchena : *Kēyūrabāhucharitra*, Hyderabad, 1966.

Peddaya, Vinnakōṭa : *Kāvyālaṅkārachūḍāmaṇī*, 7th edition, Madras, 1972.
Śrīnātha : *Sri Bhimesvarapuranamu*, Madras, 1929.
Śrīnātha : *Haravilāsamu*, Madras, 1931.
Vallabharāya, Vinukoṇḍa : *Krīḍābhirāmāmu*, Madras, 1960.
Vidyānātha : *Pratāparudrīyam*, (Sanskrit), Madras, 1927.

II. PUBLISHED WORKS :

(*i*) *English*

Altekar, A.S., *Rashtrakutas and Their Times*, Poona, 1934.

Appadorai, A., *Economic Conditions of Southern India* (*1000-1500 A.D.*), Madras, 1936.

Banerji, R.D., *History of Orissa*, 2 Volumes, Calcutta.

Fleet, J.F., *Dynasties of the Kanarese Districts* (Bombay Gazetteer, Vol. I, Part 110, Bombay, 1896.

Ganguly, D.C., *Eastern Chalukyas*, Banaras, 1937.

Gharpure, J.R., *The Mitakshara of Vijnanesvara*, Ist Edition, Bombay, 1920.

Gopalakrishna Murty, S., *Jain Vestiges in Andhra*, Hyderabad, 1963.

Handiqui, K.K., *Yasastilaka and Indian Culture*, 2nd edition, Sholapur, 1968.

Hanumantha Rao, B.S.L., *Religion in Āndhra*, Guntur, 1973.

Iswaradutt, K., *Inscriptional Glossary of Andhra Pradesh*, Hyderabad, 1963.

Majumdar, R.C., *Corporate Life in Ancient India*, 2nd edition, Calcutta, 1920.

Mahalingam T.V., *Administration and Social Life Under Vijayanagar*, 2nd edition, Madras, Part I, 1969, Part II, 1976.

Narasimha Rao, R., *Corporate Life in Medieval Andhradesa*, Secunderabad, 1967.

Nilakanta Sastri, K.A., *A History of South India*, 3rd edition, Oxford, 1971.

Parabrahma Sastry, P.V., *The Kakatiyas of Warangal*, Hyderabad, 1978.

Radhakrishna, B., *Early Telugu Inscriptions*, Hyderabad, 1971.

Ramachandra Rao, C.V., *Administration and Society in Medieval Andhra* (*A.D. 1038-1538*), *under the Later Eastern Gangas and the Suryavamsi Gajapatis*, Nellore, 1976.

Rama Rao, M., *Eastern Chalukyan Temples in Andhradesa*, Hyderabad, 1964.

Saletore, B.A., *Social and Political Life in the Vijayenagar Empire*, 2 volumes, Madras, 1934.

Satyanarayana, K., *A Study of History and Culture of the Andhras*, Vol. I, New Delhi, 1975.

Sewell, R., *List of Antiquarian Remains in the Presidency of Madras*, Vol. I, Madras, 1882.

——'List of Inscriptions and Sketches of the Dynasties of Southern India', Madras, 1884.

Sivaramamurti, C., "The Early Chalukyan Sculpture", Madras, 1960.

Somasekhara Sarma, M., *History of the Reddi Kingdoms* (Circa 1325 A.D. to Circa 1448 A.D.), Waltair, 1948.

——, *A Forgotten Chapter of Andhra History*, Waltair, 1945.

Subrahmanyam, R., *The Suryavamsi Gajapatis of Orissa*, Waltair, 1957.

Sundaram, K., *Studies in Economic and Social Conditions of Medieval Andhra* (*A.D. 1000-1600*) Machilipatam, 1968.

——, *The Simhachalam Temple*, Waltair, 1969.

Venkataramanayya, N., *The Eastern Chāḷukyas of Vēṅgī*, Madras, 1950.

——, *The Chāḷukyas of L (V)ēmulavāḍa*, Hyderabad, 1953.

Venkata Rao, N., *Lives of Telugu Poets*, Madras, 1958.

Venkata Krishna Rao, B., *History of Eastern Chalukyas of Vengi*, Hyderabad, 1973.

Vaidehi Krishna Moorthy, A., *Social and Economic Conditions in Eastern Deccan* (*From A.D. 1000-1250*), Secunderabad, 1970.

Yazdani, G. (Ed.), *The Early History of the Deccan*, 2 volumes, Oxford, 1960.

(*ii*) *Telugu*

Arudra, Samagra Āndhra Sāhityam, Series of Volumes, Madras, 1965.

Hanumantha Rao, B.S.L., *Āndhrula Charitra*, Guntur, 1983.

Hanumantha Rao, D., *Śrī Rājarājēśvara Charitamu*, Vēmulavāḍa, 1963.

Iswaradutt, K., *Prāchīnāndhra Chāritraka Bhūgōḷamu*, Hyderabad, 1963.

Krishna Rao, B.V.(Ed.) *Rājarājanarēndrapaṭṭābhishēka Sañchika*, Rajahmundry, 1922.

——, *Rājarājanarēndruḍu*, Rajahmundry, 1922.

Lakshmana Rao, K.V., *Lakshmaṇarāya Vyāsāvaḷi*, 2nd edition, Vijayawada, 1965.

Pratapareddi, S., *Āndhrula Sānghika Charitra*, Hyderabad, 1950.

Parabrahma Sastry, P.V., *Telugu Śāsanālu*, Hyderabad, 1975.

Rama Rao, M. (Ed.), *Kākatīya Sañchika*, Rajahmundry, 1935.

Seshayya, Chaganti, *Āndhra Kavitaranginṇi*. Series of Volumes, 2nd edition, Kapilesvarapuram, 1960.

Somasekhara Sarma, M., *Chāritraka Vyāsamulu*, Madras, 1950.

——(ed.), *Telgu Vijñāna Sarvasvamu*, Vol. II, Madras, 1959.

Satyanarayana, K. *Āndrula Saṁskṛiti Charitra*, 2 volumes. Hyderabad, 1981.

Virabhadra Rao. C., *Āndhrula Charitra*, 3 parts, Madras, 1910-12.

Venkataramanayya, D., *Āndhra Vangmayāraṁbhadaśa*, 2 volumes, Hyderabad, 1960.

Venkataramanayya, N., *Pallavulu-Chāḷukyulu*, Madras, 1969.

Venkatarao, N., *Āndhra Karṇaṭaka Sārasvatamulu-Paraspara Prabhāvamu*, Madras, 1962.

III. SELECT JOURNALS

(*i*) *English*

Archaeological Studies
Indian Antiquary
Indian Historical Quarterly
Indian Culture
Journal of Andhra Historical Research Society
Journal of Andhra History of Culture
New Indian Antiquary
Proceedings of the Andhra Pradesh History Congress
Proceedings of the Indian History Congress
The Journal of Oriental Research

(*ii*) *Telugu*

Āndhra Patrika (Annuals)
Āndhra Sāhitya Parishad Patrika
Bhārati
Kinnera
Nava Bhārati
Śārada
Telugu

INDEX

Addākaligachha 6,
Addanki Inscription 10,
Ādi Mahā Bappara 2
Āditya Sarma, M.V.N. 62
Ādityas'arman 22
Aıhole Prasāsti 2
Amma I-2, 4 ; II 2, 6, 14, 15
Ammarāja I 3-5, 8, 14 ;
II 6, 7, 69
Ammaraja Vijayāditya II 9
Anantavaraman Choḍagaṅga 59
Andhredeśa 1, 2
Arnamandiṅ 6
Arikesari 28-30, 60
Aruṁbaka Plates 7
Asanpura 20-25
Ayyapayya 10

Bādāmi 2
Bādapa 7, 15
Balaka-piñchha 6
Ballāladeva Vēlabhaṭa
Boddiya 6
Bejayuḍu 9
Benerjee, R.D. 55
Bhandanāditya 3-5, 7
Bhānudeva 50, 55
Bhāskarācharya 87-88, 90, 94,
99. 100
Bhaṭṭakala 9
Bōya Chieftains 9-10
Broken Inscriptions 10

Chakrakūṭa 11, 30
Chalukya Bhima I, 3, 7, 8, 10,
13, 14 ; II 16, 40, 41
Chalukyas 1, 2, 3, 8, 38, 49,
57, 60, 61, 63-65, 95
Chāmekāṁba 6, 7
Chandena 7
Chellava 7-8
Chiṁbution grant 10
Chipurupalli plates 2

Daddara I or II 3
Dakshiṇāpātha 9
Dharmavaram 10
Druvaśarman 20
Drujjūrn grant 8
Durjaya 2

Eastern Chalukyas 1

Feroz Shah 98

Gaekwad 3
Gāmakāṁba 8
Gaṇḍanārāyaṇa 7

Gaṅga kings 50 ;
Family 52, 59, 62
Gauri 62
Grīpaschimasīma 2
Goṇṭurn 5 ; Grant 2
Govindarāja 61
Guṇagavijayāditya 3, 10, 13

Inscriptions 4, 6, 9

Jainśrāvaki 7
Jananāthapura 64
Jayasiṁha 21, 22, 24, 25, 31, 32
Jayasiṁha Vallabha I, 20, 23 ; II 20
Jinavallabha 67, 71
Joga Rao, S.V. 22

Kadeyarāga 9-10
Kāla Kaṁpa or Kota Kaṁpa 3, 5,
Kaliyarti gaṇḍa Vijayāḍityā VI, 3
Kaluchum baṟṟn grants 2, 6
Kaṇḍernvāṭi Vishāyaya 5
Karmarāshtrā 14
Karṇātaka, 1
Kaṭakarājas 2. 8-9, 13
Kallabhigaṇḍa Vijayditya IV 3
Kollern 7
Kṛishṇa 2
Krishnarāja 10
Krishna Rao, B.V. 7, 9, 11, 65
Krishna Sashtri, Rai Bahadur 23
Kubja Viśhnuvardhana 1, 2, 3, 20
Kulottuṇga Chola I, 62, 64, 69, 97
Kumāragiri 98
Kumudevandhana 76, 78-79
Kuntāditya 3
Kusumāyndha 40-41

Lakshamana Rao, K.V, 11
Lakshminararajan, Khandavalli 91
Lobhachaluka 43

Mahākāla 8
Mahāsena or Karhkeya
Mailamāṁba 44
Mallapa 8, 43
Maliyaṁpuḍi 9 ; Inscription 12
Mangales'a 2
Maṅgi 10
Masulipatnam grant 6
Matsya family 2

Nāgipoti 7-8
Nagiyaṁpudi plates 9
Nāyamāṁba 7
Nellore 11
Nirupama Dhruva 31
Nṛpakāma 7

Pallavas 11, 77
Pāṁbaṟṟn 2
Pammava 6
Paṁpa 27, 67, 71
Paṇḍaraṅga 10-13, 15-16
Parāntaka 65
Paṭṭavardhanis 2-8
Ponarigi & Chiṁbulirh plates 9
Pulakesi II 2, 31
Purshottama 52, 54-55

Rajamanendra Varma 24, 76-78, 90-91, 100
Rājarāja III 50

Rājarāgenarendra 50, 80, 88-89
Rama Rao, Marenmanda 79, 91
Raṇavik Krama Pulakēs's II, 1
Rāshṭrakūṭas 4, 10-11
Raṭṭes'a 12

Saktivarman II 51
Samasta Bhuvanāe'raya Guṇaga Vijayāditya 9
Samba Sivaramamurty, M. 51
Sāmekāṁba 7
Sankila 10
Sarvalokāsiraya gina Bhavana 6
Sastri, Dr. Parabrahma 39, 45-46
Sastri Krishna 10
Sātapūtra Inscription 13
Satyāsraya 31-31, 58-59, 61
Scholars 58
Sewell 59
Seventeen towns 88
Somadevashri 70
Somāditya 3, 5
Soma Sekhar Sarma, M. 30-31, 62, 69, 72
Sundaram, K, 92

Table of the mudigoṇda Chalukyan family 41-42
Telugu people 1
Text of the Chālukyan Inscription 25
Text of the Iascription 32-36, 46-47, 80-85

Tribhuvanānkuśṇḍu 9
Tribhuvanmalla Vikramāditya VI 37
Trikaliṅga 9
Tuṁbura 8
Tuṇḍka 8

Uggivelagauḍu 3

Vallabhi 3
Varma, G.R. 89
Vasavi Kanya 88
Vedas 66
Velahargaṇa 6
Veṅgichalukyan Government 9
Veṅgī Chaiukyas 4, 11
Veṅgīmaṇḍala 2
Vengināḍu 2 ; Throne 3
Venkataramanyya, N. 10, 12, 13, 24, 27-29, 31
Venkatavadhaṁ ; Divakarla 13
Vigayāditya 50, 59-61 ; IV, 4, 13, 52 ; Ammarāga II 6
Vinayāditya yuddhamalla 28, 29, 31-32
Virabhadra Rao, Chalukuri 89
Viranarsiṁha I 53
Viriyāla Malla 37
Vishuvardhana 58-59, 71, 76-78, 87, 89-90, 100 ; Ammargñga I 3
Vishvanatha 52, 55

Yama 5
Yasodadevi, V. 52, 54, 59, 79